'20

Hey Chris,

I appreciate your friendship, rumor and heart to build and expand God's Kingdom. You're a front line leader and I'm blessed to serve with you in Church Boom. I pray this book will add to you.

Blessings,

Kenneth

HELPING OTHERS WIN

HELPING OTHERS WIN

10 Keys To Effective Mentoring

Kenneth Mulkey

Xulon Press

Xulon Press
2301 Lucien Way #415
Maitland, FL 32751
407.339.4217
www.xulonpress.com

Unless otherwise noted, Scripture is taken from the New King James Version (NKJV). Copyright © 1982 by Thomas Nelson, Inc. Used by permission. All rights reserved.

Scripture quotations marked NLT are taken from the Holy Bible, New Living Translation, copyright © 1996, 2004, 2015 by Tyndale House Foundation. Used by permission of Tyndale House Publishers, Inc., Carol Stream, Illinois 60188. All rights reserved.

Scripture quotations designated ESV are from The Holy Bible, English Standard Version ®, copyright © 2001 by Crossway Bibles, a publishing ministry of Good News Publishers. Used by permission. All rights reserved.

Printed in the United States of America.

ISBN-13: 978-1-6312-9986-5

This book is dedicated to the millions who need a mentor in their lives and the millions who will answer the call to mentor and help others win.

To the memory of Lakers legend Kobe Bryant, who dedicated himself to mentoring his daughters, current NBA players, athletes in all sports, and upcoming generations to become their best.

Table of Contents

Foreword

High five to Pastor Ken Mulkey for nailing a three-point shot with a swish to win the game with this book on the subject of mentoring. First, I love the title *Helping Others Win*. He could have titled the book "Helping You Win," but just like his quote from William Booth, the founder of the Salvation Army, this book is about others, and his mindset is to help people through this book.

I've known Ken for more than twenty years. I've observed him from afar, and I've seen him up close, and here's what I can say: Ken is what the old people would call "good people". Some people can preach well. Some can write well. But the greatest question is: can you live well? If the answer is yes, then your preaching and writing are truly successful. That's what Ken does and is. I've read quite a bit on the subject of mentoring, but I have to say this is by far the most practical, relevant, and thorough teaching on mentoring. He touches on every question, consideration, responsibility, and truth of mentoring. He leaves no unanswered questions and there is no lack of understanding or interpretation of what he means. He nailed it.

Today's younger generation is full of potential and many of them have questions surrounding the subject of mentoring, such as: what is a mentor? Who will mentor me? Where do I find a mentor? Why do I need mentoring? That may be because this is a fatherless generation that is longing and looking for superheroes. This is why comedies and Marvel movies are such blockbusters because we are looking for guides, counselors, advisers, encouragers, and heroes in our lives who will not hurt us, harm us, neglect us, or abuse us.

We could heal the ills and woes of society if more people stepped up to the plate and took on the challenge and the responsibility of mentoring those in our houses, our jobs, our churches, our relationships, and anyone else who needs answers or help. A mentor doesn't have to fix people or tell them what to do or not to do. The greatest mentors are good listeners who tell you who you are and what you can be. This is a developed skill that takes time and patience. It is not for the weary at heart, but for Christ followers who have taken Jesus's words in Matthew 28 soberly and seriously and "will make disciples of all men".

I wonder how much better our world could be if people had the courage to be transparent and vulnerable in sharing their lives, their victories and failures, their heartaches and sorrows, their pains and regrets, and their joys and loves with the next generation so they can make better choices and decisions.

You cannot have success without successors. Your goal should be not to depart this world until you have left something behind that will outlive you. You can't call your life completed until someone is ready to take the baton from your hand to theirs by the love and the investment you have made in their lives.

I don't want to go to Heaven, be embraced by Jesus in an awesome moment of intimacy, and then have Jesus look behind me and ask, "Who followed you here? Who did you mentor? Who did you invest in? Who did you spend your time with?" As we grow older, we should bring a new generation alongside of us to share our wisdom and experience.

Pastor Diego Mesa
Abundant Living Family Church

Acknowledgments

Although I'm the author of this book, there are many others who contributed to its inspiration and completion.

I would like to thank my wife, Angel, for her support and prayers; my three daughters, whose understanding gave me time and space to write.

Special thanks to Antracia Moorings and Jenn Monteagudo for their writing and literary expertise. To Steve and Jena Nielsen for their passion and contribution to the discussion questions; to Keven Griffin for his insightful critique on the sequence and feel for the readers. To Lisa Evans of the Orangewood Foundation, for her insightful thoughts and questions on mentoring; and to; Peter Vanacore of the Christian Association of Mentoring (CAYM) for sharing his best practices with me and Julius Lewis of *house_of_detail* on Instagram for his front cover design.

To my friend, Pastor Diego Mesa, for his encouragement and writing the foreword.

Can I write a book about mentoring without thanking the mentors in my life? So, I say thank you to Coach Barry Sher who believed I could go on to play college ball while I was in sixth grade; to Cardale Tademy, who gave me my first

Bible, which has given me the faith I possess today; to Bishop Sheridan McDaniel, for exposing me to worship, street ministry, and opportunities to preach; to Harold Keeling, who took me under his wing as a friend and teammate at SCU; to Pastor Larry Matteson, who gave me the opportunity to train people for ministry; to Dennis Lauderdale, who provided the necessary wisdom to battle attorneys and deal with judges; to Pastor Bayless Conley, whose example, teaching and friendship have always encouraged me; and to my parents, Elton (deceased) and Vera Mulkey, whose love and sacrifice laid the foundation for serving others.

Preface

If you read my first book, *Run To Win: Finding Your Lane and Finishing*, you discovered God has a purpose for your life. I outlined clear steps to help you discover and begin to execute His purpose in your life. Knowing your "why" provides the rhyme and reason for your existence in a way that nothing else in life can. When you begin to run in your lane, or live in your purpose, with His divine power energizing you, it's like discovering a treasure and then enjoying the benefits of its riches. You become a wealthy person.

Running your race—or serving God with the gifts and talents He's given you—is your target. If you faithfully pursue this throughout your life, then you will finish your course here on earth and, like the aged apostle Paul, will be able to say, "I have fought the good fight, I have finished my race, I have kept the faith" (2 Tim. 4:7-8).

Yet, it is impossible to run your race in life to the finish and win without serving others and helping them to grow and live in their purpose. This is winning. This idea is profoundly communicated by General William Booth, the founder of the Salvation Army.

The one-word telegram by Jay McCarl:

It was Christmas Eve, 1910. General William Booth, the founder of the Salvation Army, was an invalid and near the end of his life—it was impossible for him to attend the Army's annual convention.

Someone suggested that Booth send a telegram to be read at the opening of the convention to the many Salvation Army soldiers in attendance, as an encouragement for their many hours of labor serving others throughout the holidays and the cold winter months. Booth agreed.

Funds were limited and telegrams charged by the word, so to ensure as much money as possible would still go to help the needy, General Booth decided to send a one word message. He searched his mind and reviewed his years of ministry, seeking the one word that would summarize his life and the mission of the Army, as well as encourage the soldiers to continue on.

When the thousands of delegates met, the moderator announced that Booth could not be present due to his failing health. Gloom and pessimism swept across the convention floor until the moderator announced that Booth had sent a telegram to be read at the start of the first session. He opened the message and read just one word:

"Others!"

This word "others" requires us to take the focus off of ourselves, our wants, and our needs, and place attention on someone else. A life well lived is one that sees and serves others. The most valuable resource on the earth is not oil, platinum, gold, or silver, but people. This is why Jesus left a perfect heaven to dwell on the earth He created and be with people, even though they were often against Him. "For even the Son of Man did not come to be served, but to serve, and to give his life as a ransom for many" (Mark 10:45).

The varying needs of people can only be met by those who are willing to serve. We all know the enjoyment of being served. When someone does something for you, whether significant or small, it enhances your life in the moment and brings fulfillment to a current or ongoing need.

There is a nice hotel property on the coast of Southern California that my wife Angel and I love to frequent. This location is amazing, the food is delicious (best key lime pie I've ever had!) and the accommodations are comfortable. Any of these qualities are desirable enough to make you want to stay there, yet the most outstanding quality that attracts us to this place is the service. The friendly staff always makes us feel like we belong there, takes the time to answer questions, and goes the extra mile. No matter how great the food, location, and shops, if the customer service was bad, our first time there would've been our last.

My mother, Vera Mulkey, is someone whom I've seen embody this concept of serving. I've watched her tirelessly serve our family, friends, community, and church decade after decade. Whether money was given or thank you's were not—she has served. I've heard her say, "the secret of living is giving." This statement was passed down to her from my grandmother, Lorene Smith, who lived out the truth: "It is more blessed to give than to receive" (Acts 20:35).

Life is not just about receiving, but about giving and serving. A life motivated by selfish ambition becomes small and self-destructive. The term *erithea* from the Greek language describes a person only concerned with his own welfare, susceptible to being bribed, or a self-willed person who seeks opportunity for promotion. This person would resort to any method for winning followers, even if it were morally or ethically wrong. This reminds me of King David's son, Absalom, who manipulated and deceived the people in order to win them as followers (2 Sam. 15:1-10). This is why the Apostle Paul said in Philippians 2:3-4 (NIV), "Do nothing out of selfish ambition or vain conceit. Rather in humility value others above yourselves..."

The man who thinks too much about himself thinks too little of others. Selfish ambition shrinks your potential and limits your ability to relate to people and experience a genuine empathy and sympathy for them. Serving the needs of others, however, expands your life, and as you help someone else it recharges, renews, and revives your heart and soul.

Serving is how you release greatness. Dr. Martin Luther King Jr. said, "Everybody can be great because anybody can serve. You don't have to have a college degree to serve. You don't have to make your subject and verb agree to serve. You only need a heart full of grace, a soul generated by love."

Jesus put an exclamation point on serving others just hours before He was sentenced to death by crucifixion. It demonstrates just how much He wanted the message and modeling of serving to be etched in their memories. This is the heart behind this book—and there is guaranteed blessing in making service a practice of life.

Thus, in the following chapters, you'll discover how to effectively serve by becoming a mentor to others.

Key No. 1

Mentoring Begins With You

"Man, my knees are shaking!" I said these words to my best man as we stood at the altar awaiting the entrance of the bridal party and my bride, Angel. This had never happened to me before in my life—my knees shaking—despite the fact that I'd been in situations where they should have, but didn't. It was involuntary and reminded me of scenes from television comedies. I was about to exchange wedding vows, making one of the most life-altering commitments ever. In that moment, I discovered it mattered who was standing next to me on that special day. I counted myself blessed to have many close friends, some even like brothers, but Cardale was not just a friend to me—he was my mentor.

I met him when I was in ninth grade, at the Pacific Coast Highway campus of Long Beach City College. Back then, young people would gather at the college in the summer to engage in constructive activities while we were not in school. The activity I engaged in the most was basketball. I loved playing basketball and still do. We always had a great time playing, competing and even talking trash to one another.

Cardale was one of the camp counselors, and took a special interest in me. He later shared some of the qualities he observed in me: my commitment to basketball, passion for the game, drive to succeed, tenacity; he said I was a silent destroyer with a no-nonsense demeanor, and a get-the-job-done kind of guy. Wow! I feel like I should pay him for saying all of those nice things about me. (The truth is, a mentor will always see things in a mentee that a mentee may not see or acknowledge about himself.) A mentor can articulate what he observes and even the potential that exists. When Jesus first met one of His disciples, named Nathanael, He said, "Behold, an Israelite indeed, in whom is no deceit!" (John 1:47). He said something about Nathanael that perhaps no one had ever said before.

During this camp, Cardale and I connected. There was no special formula. We played basketball, went to basketball games, and talked about life. He shared his insights on girls, community issues, and even his past mistakes. He kept it real with me and I kept it real with him. He visited my home and got to know my parents and siblings, and soon it was like he was part of the family. I became acquainted with his family as well—in particular his mother, Ms. Mary. Cardale, also followed my high school basketball career, which eventually earned me a full athletic scholarship to play basketball for Santa Clara University. He saw me when I played well and when I played poorly, but was always honest, positive, and encouraging. Cardale was present at one of the biggest and most exciting high school games of my career.

This game was like a modern-day David versus Goliath. I attended a small parochial school in Long Beach called St. Anthony's, and on this day we were playing against Poly High, known nationwide for their dominance in basketball. We'd had a tremendous season progressing to and through the CIF Southern Section Playoffs to eventually face a very formidable opponent. But this game was personal. I knew all the players at Poly from playing on All-Star teams and the community, making this game exciting. In three years of playing varsity basketball, St. Anthony's had never beaten Poly or even come close. Ironically, Poly was Cardale's alma mater.

The stage was set and the battle began. We were a small but well-coached team with great camaraderie, as most of us had been playing together since the ninth grade. The game went into triple overtime. With everything on the line, I made some big plays down the stretch and we won. It was one of the most historic and memorable games for us as a team and for our school. Our little team made headline sports page news in the *Long Beach Press Telegram*. My high school teammates and I still reference that game to this day because it is forever etched in our memories. We were the underdogs and we won!

Over the years, Cardale often spoken of that game and my performance in it. He has been a constant encourager—even in my adult years—and someone who believes in me and wants me to do well. You can't put a monetary value on someone believing in and encouraging you. One thing I know for sure is every person needs encouragement, even if the individual is extremely talented or intelligent. We all need someone to believe in what we can become, even before we manifest our

potential. Encouragement is especially necessary in our forma-
tive and teenage years as we begin to discover who we are, learn
social skills, and develop our worldview.

I love this quote by Johann Wolfgang
von Goethe: "Treat people as if they
were what they ought to be and you
help them to become what they are
capable of being." This is what Cardale
did for me and other young men as
well—it's what a mentor does.

*We all need
someone to believe
in what we can
become, even
before we manifest
our potential*

As I moved on to college to pursue
my degree and to play basketball, I encountered some challenging times. It was my first time away from home, my school
classes were demanding, and basketball was not panning out like
I'd hoped. It was a big difference from high school, where I was a
superstar basketball player. In college, everyone had been a high
school superstar basketball player. Sometimes I would get angry
and call Cardale. He would calmly talk to me, find out what
was going on, and help me to settle down. It was reassuring to
know I had a go-to person; someone who knew me well, knew
what to say and how to say it in a way that made sense to me.
Another person can say the same words yet not have the same
effect, simply because that person doesn't know you as well.

In several of our conversations, Cardale would mention
the Lord and what the Bible said. He didn't do it all the time,
but when he did it felt natural—never forced or awkward.
He was just sharing about who the Lord was in his life and
I would listen intently. No one else was having this kind of
conversation with me. As I look back on this, the words he

shared were watering seeds that had been planted. Before I went away to college, he gave me a paperback edition of the Good News Bible. It was an easier translation to read than the King James Version. I sat it on my desk but I do not remember ever picking it up to read. My school work, basketball practice, and socializing took up much of my time, and the Bible wasn't on my list of priorities.

Every summer when I returned home, Cardale and I would connect. We would catch up on life and talk about basketball in the college ranks and professionally and work out with other players who were in college at the same time.

In my senior year of college, I remember staying in my dorm room one Saturday night as opposed to going out. The school year was coming to an end and I was thinking deeply about what my next steps would be. Would I remain in Northern California? Would I go overseas to play basketball professionally in Germany? What would I do? The thought of going back home to Long Beach to help my parents and encourage other young men who played sports to get their education was at the forefront of my thoughts. As I contemplated what career I would venture into, so many thoughts rushed to the forefront of my mind; then I distinctly remember thinking, "I want to do something to help people." I did not fully understand in that very moment that God was speaking to me about His calling and purpose in my life. After that thought came, I picked up the Good News Bible that had sat on my desk for years and began to read.

I was not a Christian at that time, but God was definitely drawing me to Himself, and one of His key vessels was my friend and mentor Cardale. As I think back on my journey to becoming a Christian and doing what I was born to do in the world and in God's kingdom, I see the value of having a mentor. One of the things that stood out in my relationship with Cardale was that he initiated the relationship. He saw something in me that led us to connect.

Initiation on behalf of the mentor is crucial in the beginning of a mentoring relationship. I don't know how the relationship would've been different if I pursued it and he was disinterested. Honestly, I doubt I would have initiated the friendship beyond the normal interactions we had. It was the initiative coming from him that set the stage.

Another important fact is that Cardale has always been himself. He is a secure man. He didn't put on airs and try to be someone he wasn't. He was able to interact with young kids from all backgrounds with humility, and that's what made him cool. The qualities he possessed made him liked by many of the other young guys because we needed good male role models in the African-American community. Additionally, over the years I observed his interaction with people from different races, ethnicities, ages, and socio-economic backgrounds, and in all of them, he was the same. You don't have to force yourself to act or dress young if that's not who you are. Being the authentic and best version of yourself will be the true source of connection in the mentor-mentee relationship.

Cardale always encouraged me while giving me the truth about situations, so I could think them through clearly. He proved himself to be a friend. As playing basketball increased my popularity in high school, it would have been easy for him to manipulate the relationship to benefit his personal goals and interests, but he never did. He simply cared about me and other young people in the community. He has also worked with young people in other communities around the United States. I'm amazed at how God opens up doors for him, granting him favor in different cities with young people in need. He has a gift for rolling up his sleeves, connecting with people, caring for them, speaking truth, and turning things around for good. All of this is part of God's calling on his life, and he has obeyed what the Lord has given him to do. In short, he's helped others win. This calling is not exclusive to Cardale alone, but is something all of us can do. His goal has not been about obtaining the best jobs, making the most money, living in the most prestigious neighborhoods, or driving the best cars; instead, his life's aim exceeds material possessions. He has helped me by living above reproach, believing my life had a larger purpose, and being a friend through good times and bad.

I've been preaching the gospel now for more than thirty years. I've been blessed to pastor, lead, and speak to thousands of people about Jesus in different parts of the world. Yet, one of the strongest beats of my heart is mentoring and developing others to become everything they have been created to be and called to do. I want to help you do the same. You carry within you an enormous amount of God-given, unrealized, and untapped potential that is to be lived out and released to better the lives of others. You are reading this book because you believe you have so much more to give, and you can make a difference by helping others win. The way you can do it is through mentoring.

Reflection Questions

1. Who was the most influential mentor in your life?

2. How did that mentor make you feel about the possibilities for your life?

3. What did this mentor instill in you, and how has that made you a better person?

4. What would you tell your mentor about his/her influence in your journey?

My Prayer...

Lord, help me to faithfully impart to others what You have given me.

Key No. 2

Understanding the Purpose of Mentoring

I t's always helpful to understand what something is not before you understand what something is. This is why cashiers learn what counterfeit money and fake IDs look like. This also applies to mentoring. A mentor is not your counselor, therapist, consultant, or coach. Some of the elements that each of these experts utilize may appear in the course of a mentoring relationship. This may happen if the mentor functions in any of the above. However, your mentee may acquire the services of one of these while in the process of being mentored by you. This can occur because there are distinctions amongst these professions that are all geared to help the individual.

The main dysfunction every mentor strongly avoids is codependency. This is characterized by a person looking to you to meet all their emotional needs, answer all their questions, and be available at their beck and call. This is unhealthy and must not be allowed to happen. Co-dependency leads to you becoming 'god' to this person, which is a responsibility you were not meant to carry. This is why you always point the person you are mentoring to God. If co-dependent behavior begins to manifest, have an honest conversation to immediately correct this or discontinue mentoring this person.

Baseball fans may remember Cal Ripken Jr., known as "the Iron Man of baseball". Ripken played in the major league for twenty-one years, in 2,632 consecutive games. He was one of only seven players to amass 400 home runs and over 3,000 hits. The first day Ripken played in the majors, he got three hits right away, then fell into a horrible slump. For a while, he felt like he just could not hit the ball. Another player on the team named Eddie Murray, who was about five years older than Ripken, had experienced a similar slump early on in his career. Murray put his arm around Ripkin and said just five simple words: "It's going to be okay."

Ripken says of that moment, "The value of a mentor... I don't know what value you can place on it. But the right words spoken at the right time from a person that's been through it before, can make all the difference in your school year, can make all the difference in that youth game. It's a very personal feeling. When you help somebody, there is a sense of satisfaction, gratification that comes over you, that cannot be equaled, even if you hit the game-winning home run."

In order to understand mentoring, it would be helpful to look at its origin. The word mentor comes from the name of a character in the classic epic poem *The Odyssey* by the Greek poet Homer. In the poem, the character Mentor was both friend and counselor to Odysseus. While fighting in the Trojan War, Odysseus, king of Ithaca, entrusts the care of his household to Mentor, who serves as teacher and overseer of Odysseus's son, Telemachus.

After the war, Odysseus returns home to find his son Telemachus has grown into a man under the wisdom and guidance of "Mentor." From this poem, the word mentor took on the meaning of a trusted advisor, friend, teacher and wise person who instructs and encourages another to develop skills that lead to influence and success.

History is full of examples of mentoring relationships: Socrates and Plato, Aristotle and Alexander the Great, Hayden and Beethoven, Freud and Jung. Even the Bible features a number of mentoring relationships that provide helpful models to draw from.

Different Types of Mentoring

Before I progress into the key distinctions that will help you grasp what mentoring is about, it will be helpful to understand the different types of mentoring.

The type of mentoring that is the primary goal of this book is called **Direct Mentoring**. This describes relational, face-to-face development, and is the most optimal type in my opinion. We live in a time where we can FaceTime one another and participate in Zoom video conferencing meetings, but there is nothing like eye-to-eye contact, non-verbal communication, and simply being fully present.

The other type of mentoring that takes place (often unbeknownst to you as a mentor) is **Indirect Mentoring**. This happens when you are being yourself and living out your strengths and passions. A person who is hungry to learn and is able to regularly hear you speak, watch you work, and watch you serve is indirectly learning from you without your knowledge. This person is taking mental notes of your demeanor, expertise, and interpersonal skills, among other things. This "indirect mentee" is digesting information and applying what is gleaned without ever speaking to you. When this occurs, the light of God in you is shining on them and teaching them lessons their hearts are longing for.

This reminds me of a nice young man at my former church who was called into the preaching ministry. We were cordial and spoke occasionally, but I couldn't say we were close. Years after I transitioned from that church by God's leading, I would be invited back to speak. While conversing with church members after service, I learned this young man had adopted my speaking style. This was news to me. Indirect mentees will often emulate someone when venturing into a new vocation or position.

The third type of mentoring is what I call **Multiple Mentoring**. King Solomon speaks of this idea in Proverbs 11:14 (NLT): "...there is safety in having many advisers." Even well-seasoned mentors have blind spots and any mentor worth his or her salt will agree with this statement. One of the young men I mentor (I'll call him John to protect his identity) has other mentors as well. I'm fully aware of who the other mentors are and I'm not threatened. Oftentimes, the mentee recognizes specific qualities in each mentor that are essential to his growth and development. One mentor may help him with personal financial management; another with goal setting; another with leadership skills while another with spiritual disciplines. Does this make sense to you? In this type of mentoring, the mentee demonstrates initiative in most of these relationships because of his awareness of what areas of his life require growth. Since he cannot grow alone, he seeks mentors.

The final type of mentoring is called **Reverse Mentoring** or **Mutual Mentoring**. In the Greek mythological story of Mentor, the story centers around an older man helping a young boy, Telemachus, to develop into a man. The key subjects of the story demonstrate the process of maturity and growth over a period of time. The truth is, there are some areas in the life of a mentor that the mentee can assist with. There is great potential in your mentee, so is it strange that there are some things you can learn as a mentor? Isn't it true that even parents can learn some things from their children?

One example that comes to mind is technology. Millennials and Gen Z (1996 and after) have grown up with a phone in their hands and use technology for most every experience of life: shopping, traveling, education, transportation, entertainment, the list goes on and on. Those of us who are over forty years old (wink-wink) utilize technology in many of the same ways, but for those thirty-five and younger, it is second nature.

Have you ever experienced the following scenario? You discover your iPhone is not working and you don't know why. You're trying to correct the issue without success. Your fifteen-year-old child sees you're in a frenzy, takes your phone, accesses some top-secret undetectable icon and with a few swift thumb movements—voila—it's fixed!

I was conducting a leadership training for a church team of staff and volunteers when the subject of reaching the younger generation came up. Some of the forty-plus-year-old attendees came to realize they could connect with the younger generations via technology and social media. How would a nineteen-year-old feel if a forty-two-year-old asked for their help in discovering how to better use their computer or how to locate certain apps? The connection point will be an organic entry way into how you both could learn from one another.

John Daresh, professor of educational leadership at the University of Texas at El Paso, offered this guidance: "A mentor does not necessarily have to be an older person who is ready, willing and able to provide all of the answers to those who are newcomers. Usually, mentors have a lot of experience and craft knowledge to share with others."

If you're open, teenagers and young adults can help you understand the mindset, attitudes, and challenges of their generation. They can provide you with a Sociology 101 course on what's really happening with our young people today. If you're going to mentor them, you must get a better understanding of them.

Developing Others

At its core, mentoring is about developing others. It's developmental. So, a mentor is someone you can learn from in order to grow and develop into the person God designed you to be. Imagine a piece of undeveloped land in front of you. It has unlimited potential and the sky's the limit on ideas for what to construct on it. But there is a cost involved. Developing land doesn't happen overnight, and it isn't free. The cost in developing others can be one of the tasks you choose to avoid, but the rewards you see in the lives of others and the sense of deep satisfaction are incomparable. To develop means to grow, to make or become bigger, better, and more useful.

Before you develop others, you need to make sure you are continuing to develop yourself by applying the Four R's of Personal Development:

1. Reading - The Bible and other books.
2. Relationships - People who you relate to and help you grow.
3. Resources - D.I.S.C. Test, Strength Finder.
4. Risks - Trying new things.

According to research from Thomas Crowley, 85 percent of self-made millionaires read two or more books per month.[1] The reason they read is to grow and learn for self-improvement. A large part of developing yourself is staying connected to God by reading the Bible. According to the Barna Group, readership of the Bible in the United States is 34%, which is astoundingly low[2] considering the average home has four Bibles. John 15:4-5 offers wisdom on staying plugged into God:

---

[1] Crowley, Thomas C. "How Many Books Does the Average Self-Made Millionaire Read?" *Rich Habits: The Key to Success and a Happy Future* (blog) June 22, 2015; https://richhabits.net/how-many-books-does-the-average-self-made-millionaire-read/.

[2] State of the Bible 2018: Seven Top Findings, The Barna Group, July 10, 2018; https://www.barna.com/research/state-of-the-bible-2018-seven-top-findings/.

"Abide in Me, and I in you. As the branch cannot bear
fruit of itself, unless it abides in the vine, neither can
you, unless you abide in Me. I am the vine, you are the
branches. He who abides in Me, and I in him, bears
much fruit; for without Me you can do nothing."

Reading books for leisure is a good exercise for our mind
and is enjoyable. But I'm talking about selecting an area where
you need growth and finding some good books to read on the
topic. Set a target to read at least one book per month. This
will increase your knowledge, understanding and wisdom.

Next, you need to have close, healthy friendships with
others where you are receiving input. In my personal experience, I've observed that women tend to practice this very
well. Not all of your relationships have to be "close", but rest
assured we all need trusted individuals whom we can confide
in and who can sharpen us.

As it relates to resources, there are several available if you
search. A few I would recommend are D.I.S.C. (Dominance,
Influence, Steadiness, Compliance) Assessments, which help
you understand more about your personality traits. Go to
www.discprofile.com.

The Strength Finder 2.0 is an assessment that will help you
locate your top five strengths. This can assist you in playing to
your strengths, as opposed to just avoiding your weaknesses.
Go to www.gallupstrengthcenter.com.

Finally, do something new or expand and enlarge something you have been doing. Take a step. Stretch yourself.
Developing oneself leads to the natural byproduct of developing others. Both are a calling to you from God.

This is the bedrock of Jesus's life. There is no advancement without the development of others in business, ministry or life. When you develop others it creates a ripple effect, touching the lives of family, friends, and beyond. Further, you are growing the mission/vision of the church or organization you are part of. When you mentor, you facilitate people's growth in purpose (why you do), priorities (when you do), principles (how to do), and practices (what to do).

Modeling for Others

Jesus was a model to the disciples, which is why He said, "Follow me." This language was echoed by Paul in the following verses: "Imitate me, just as I also imitate Christ" (1 Cor. 11:1) and again in Philippians 3:17, "Join with others in following my example, brothers, and take note of those who live according to the pattern we gave you."

According to Dr. Albert Mehrabian, Professor Emeritus of Psychology at University of California Los Angeles, people learn fifty-five percent of information by what they see. As a model or example, your actions, speech, and spirit are duplicatable to those you mentor. For example, if a leader models harsh tones when speaking, is demanding, and doesn't listen, the mentee who is learning from him by watching and listening will repeat this behavior. Paul knew the importance of this concept, which is why he passed it on to Timothy.

> Let no one despise your youth, but be an example to the believers in word, in conduct, in love, in spirit, in faith, in purity. (1 Timothy 4:12)

A mentor helps others "become" by a process. There are series of steps that occur in the mentoring relationship—it is by no means an instantaneous process. Think of the process of baking a cake. There is a recipe you follow and each step must be done in order. You can't mix the ingredients until you have gathered them in the bowl and you can't put the cake in the oven if you don't have all the ingredients. Jesus told His disciples, "Follow me and I will make you become fishers of men" (Mark 1:17). Jesus is the epitome and the divine personification of a mentor, so we should learn from Him. He has established a model to follow of helping others "become."

> *Jesus is the epitome and the divine personification of a mentor, so we should learn from Him*

Steps to Helping Someone "Become"

- **Invitation:** This is where you invite someone into your life by allowing them into your space. Mentors are typically the initiator of the invitation. You're opening up the door to your world, your thought processes, your activities and your experiences. This is not to say when someone asks you to mentor them, or help them develop, it won't work—it has and will. Often times though, the mentor is more likely to see the potential for growth and development in the mentee before the mentee themselves see it. Jesus initiated when He told the disciples to follow Him. Elijah was the initiator in his relationship with Elisha. It was Paul who approached Timothy and took him along.

- **Information**: Learning what you don't know, doing something you have not done, becoming someone you've not been. There cannot be any growth or development without providing knowledge. It's a vital key to power and freedom. A person can only 'be' better and 'do' better if he 'knows' better. You do not have to know everything—none of us do—but share what you've learned. This is a core principle in discipleship (Matt. 28:20).

- **Observation**: People can learn by hearing, but they will always learn more by observing. The thing(s) you want someone to do will be more easily grasped if they can look at you as you're doing it. This is known as "shadowing." Many a time I've gone to my bank or credit union to transact business and seen two tellers at the window helping me: the experienced teller who was watching and the trainee who was helping me. Seeing how to talk to customers and satisfy their requests is as essential as any textbook training. Jesus knew this.

And Jesus went about all Galilee, teaching in their synagogues, preaching the gospel of the kingdom, and healing all kinds of sickness and all kinds of disease among the people. Then His fame went throughout all Syria; and they brought to Him all sick people who were afflicted with various diseases and torments, and

those who were demon-possessed, epileptics, and para-
lytics; and He healed them. (Matthew 4:23-24)

The only way Jesus's disciples were able to witness Him
preaching and healing was for Him to get out and do it. It's
one thing to share a book or story with someone, but it's quite
another for them to see it in action.

- **Participation**: Benjamin Franklin said, "Tell me and
  I forget; teach me and I may remember; involve me
  and I learn." This is exactly what Jesus did. Upon
  seeing the multitudes and being moved with compassion for them, He gave His disciples the opportunity to participate. He told them to pray to the Lord
  to send out laborers into His harvest (Matt. 9:38).
  He then delegated His authority to them to preach,
  heal, and deliver those possessed with demons. They
  were sent on a two-week mission trip to their Jewish
  countrymen and became the answer to the prayer for
  laborers (Matt. 10:1, 7-8). Jesus gave these young men
  a calculated measure of participation that included
  instructions on what to do and how to respond when
  things didn't go as planned. This two-week excursion
  would be the first step to them one day taking the
  gospel to the world.

- **Multiplication**: The mentoring model Jesus established was not to end with the twelve disciples. His goal
  was for the model to be duplicated many times over
  from individual to individual and from generation to

generation. This is called multiplication. "Go therefore and make disciples of all the nations, baptizing them in the name of the Father and of the Son and of the Holy Spirit, teaching them to observe all things that I have commanded you; and lo, I am with you always, even to the end of the age" (Matthew 28:19-20).

Therefore, a key quality you should possess is believing and expecting the mentee to surpass you.

> Most assuredly, I say to you, he who believes in Me, the works that I do he will do also; and greater works than these he will do, because I go to My Father. (John 14:12)

In their book, *The Servant Leader*, Ken Blanchard and Phil Hodges highlight this important phenomena of duplication of oneself. "As a servant leader the way you serve the vision is by developing people so that they can work on that vision when you're not around. The ultimate sign of an effective servant leader is what happens when you are not there."

While a mentoring relationship is mutually beneficial, there is a cost involved. You are pouring into another person, so that means there will be times when you will experience fatigue and inconvenience. Don't think of this as a negative, but it's best to go into the relationship knowing there is a cost. Consider Luke 14:28-29:

> For which of you, intending to build a tower, does not sit down first and count the cost, whether he has enough to finish it— lest, after he has laid the foundation, and is not able to finish, all who see it begin to mock him, saying, 'This man began to build and was not able to finish'?

You are not trying to construct a tower, as verse 29 suggests, but you are building a disciple of Christ and a servant leader whom you will prepare to multiply in others what you have given to them. As you embark on this mentoring relationship, step back and evaluate what investments you are going to have to make and the effect it will have on your life. Mentoring will cost you in the areas of:

- time
- patience
- prayer
- thought
- resources
- emotional energy
- repetition

While the list can look overwhelming and the thought daunting, the reward of mentoring far exceeds the costs. The payoff comes when you witness God multiply the seeds you've sown. Those seeds will likely be used to plant into other mentoring relationships and many more persons will be developed.

Reflection Questions

1. What is the most important thing you've learned about mentoring?

2. How can you avoid co-dependency in the mentor/mentee relationship?

3. Why is being a good example important in mentoring?

4. What are some ways to approach a mentee for mentoring?

My Prayer...

Father, I pray that You would deeply form the character of Christ in me, so He will be seen by my mentees.

Key No. 3

You Are A Mentor

You have probably never heard of a woman named Mrs. Flowers, who once encouraged a young girl around the age of seven or eight to go into a segregated library for blacks only and read 110 books (all the books that library had). Mrs. Flowers would occasionally invite that young girl over to her house, and they would read and talk together. The young girl especially loved poetry, after having discovered it reading those 110 books, saying that "poetry is best when it comes off your lips and rolls off your tongue."

That young girl was the late Maya Angelou, renowned poet, educator, historian and actress. Angelou went on to write twelve bestsellers, yet she would always credit the mentorship of Mrs. Flowers—unknown to society, but certainly known to her for her success.

Anyone can be a mentor.

Whether you realize it or not, you have been a mentor to many—perhaps you didn't realize it. You don't have to be in a leadership position for people to observe you and glean from your life. In order for you to mentor, you first have to see yourself as one. This requires intentionality on your part. Your God-given identity enables you to mentor effectively because you are confidently working out of the wisdom of His Word and your life experiences.

> *Whether you realize it or not, you have been a mentor to many*

You might think that your lack of formal education would hinder you in mentoring, but really you do have an education. Whether through school, or self-taught, you have worthwhile experience to share.

Just going through life's ups and downs, highs and lows, has given you much value to pass on. For example, you have undoubtedly learned a great deal about how to treat and respond to people in different circumstances. Employers pay more for a team player who works well with others than someone who has all the skills but doesn't get along with the team.

In addition to your experience, you also have an endowment from heaven. You have a gift (or gifts) deposited on the inside of you by God, and they are there to share with the church and the world so that people might see Christ through you.

There is a story about a girl who was the daughter of one of the royal families of Europe; she had a big, bulbous nose that, in her eyes, destroyed her beauty and resulted in her seeing herself as an ugly person. Finally, her family hired a famous plastic surgeon to change the contour of the girl's nose. He did his work and then came the moment when the bandages were taken off so the girl could see the results. The doctor concluded that the operation had been a total success. All the ugly contours were gone and her nose was noticeably different. When the incisions healed and the redness disappeared, she would be a beautiful girl. He held up the mirror for the girl to see. But the negative self-image was so deeply embedded in the girl that when she saw herself in the mirror, she couldn't see any change. She broke into tears and cried out, "Oh, I knew it wouldn't work!"

It took six months before the girl would accept the fact that she was indeed an attractive person, and it wasn't until she accepted this fact that her self-image and behavior began to change accordingly. So it is with those who are in Christ. We must accept our new identity in Him and what He's given to us for transformation to take place.

Romans 12:2 says, "And do not be conformed to this world, but be transformed by the renewing of your mind, that you may prove what is that good and acceptable and perfect will of God." Part of walking in the plans of God for your life is having a renewed mind about how you view yourself as a child of God. Your life cannot rise to the level of God's plan for you without your thinking being aligned with His Word.

Proverbs 23:7 teaches that you are what you think— whether right or wrong, good or bad. Your words and actions are a product of what you think. You cannot be and do all God has purposed for you without thinking right thoughts about yourself.

The word *thinks* in Proverbs 23:7 is the Hebrew word *sha'ar*—it means to split or open, to act as a gatekeeper, to estimate, to set a price. When you plug that definition into the Scripture, it reads: "For as a man thinks (estimates, sets a price/value) in his heart, so is he." In other words, if you don't value yourself at the correct level, you will devalue all the good things in you. In the book *Crisis Counseling*, author Dr. H. Norman Wright says one of the ways suicidologists characterize a suicidal person is as one "who needs reassurance of self-worth in order to maintain his feelings of self-esteem." Oftentimes, we sell ourselves short in the value assessments regarding our person, purpose, contributions, and productivity, and this causes us to sell others short as well. This has a true effect on the relationships we have.

The way you see yourself is how you think and believe others will see you. In Numbers 13:31-33, spies were on a reconnaissance mission to observe the land of Canaan and bring back a report to the nation. The majority of the men who came back said, "We are not able to go up against the people, for they are stronger than we." The Scripture continues:

> And they gave the children of Israel a bad report of the land which they had spied out, saying, "The land through which we have gone as spies is a land that devours its inhabitants, and all the people whom we saw in it are men of great stature. There we saw the giants (the descendants of Anak came from the giants); and we were like grasshoppers in our own sight, and so we were in their sight.

God assured them the victory belonged to them, but they viewed themselves as grasshoppers instead of the giants they were. There had not been any dialogue with the giants at all which said, "we see you as grasshoppers." No, this perspective originated from within because they didn't believe what God had spoken, which was that He'd given His people the land. It is impossible to consistently behave in a manner that is inconsistent with the way we see ourselves.

The parable of the Good Samaritan in Luke 10:25-27 illustrates how different people view others by the way they see themselves. For example, the thieves in the parable used people and stole from others. This led them to see the man as a target and a victim. The priests and the Levites were law keepers and legalists. They viewed the man as a problem to be avoided and a sinner who probably deserved the treatment he received. The Samaritan was rejected and despised by others—so he saw the man as a person in need.

While you may understand that you are to love yourself, you may be wondering how do it. First, love God. Then, believe what God says about you. Internalize the fact that you are a new creation, the apple of His eye and more than a conqueror. Thinking the right thoughts is key. Philippians 4:8 says, "Finally, brethren, whatever things are true, whatever things are noble, whatever things are just, whatever things are pure, whatever things are lovely, whatever things are of good report, if there is any virtue and if there is anything praiseworthy—meditate on these things."

In order to be effective as a mentor, raising your relationship skills has to be a priority. Decide to put energy into being likable. How? Smile at people. Listen when others talk. Compliment and affirm the good in others. Remembering people's names is also important. Dale Carnegie, the famous writer and lecturer said, "A person's name is the sweetest sound they hear." Make a study of remembering names. When you hear someone's name, repeat it a few times in your mind. When you remember names, it's the first step in showing genuine care for others. People don't care how much you know until they know how much you care. A big part of being a mentor is focusing on the interests of others. You can make more friends in two months by becoming interested in other people than you can in two years by trying to get others people interested in you.

Another aspect of building relationships is asking people to help you. Nothing makes a person feel more important than to do something for you that you cannot do for yourself. Benjamin Franklin said, "He that has once done you a kindness will be more ready to do you another, than he whom you yourself have obliged." One of the quickest ways to develop relationships is to ask people to help you. The act of working side by side others creates camaraderie. Finally, you should bring something to the relationship. Be a person others can count on by being consistent, a person of character, and by being Christlike. Your aim is to make deposits to the relationship, not just make withdrawals.

How to Treat Others

Mentoring is a two-way relationship where you are required to engage respectfully with another. Matthew 7:12 says,

Therefore, whatever you want men to do to you, do also
to them, for this is the Law and the Prophets.

Here is a simple rule of thumb guide for behavior: ask
yourself what you want people to do for you, then grab the initiative and do it for them Here are four ways you want others
to treat you that will guide you in how to treat them as well.

1. **You want others to encourage you.** Job 4:4 says, "Your
words have upheld him who was stumbling." As you encourage
others, you make room for that encouragement to return to
you. There is no better exercise for strengthening the heart
than reaching down and lifting people up. Everyone needs
and responds to encouragement. When you uplift someone
with pure motives, it serves the person to whom it is given.
Not everybody responds to encouragement the same way, but
you can be sure they need it.

2. **You want others to appreciate you.** "The deepest craving
in human nature is the craving to be appreciated," said psychol-
ogist and philosopher William James. The need to be appreciated is an innate part of our being as humans. Take a look at
some of the reasons employees give when they're unhappy at
work: their employer fails to give them credit for suggestions;
their employer fails to correct their grievances; their employer
criticizes employees in front of others; their employer fails to
ask employees their opinions. It all often boils down to the
worker feeling like their importance is being dismissed.

Showing appreciation creates a feeling of importance that is more powerful than money, promotion, or working conditions. Appreciation paves the way to achievement because it's as if you are the wind in someone else's sails, propelling them forward.

3. **You want others to forgive you.** We all make mistakes, and those whom we mentor will as well. Remember, the two great marks of a Christian are giving and forgiving. People who refuse to forgive only hurt themselves, as they bear a burden they weren't designed to carry.

4. **You want others to listen to you.** People appreciate the gift of listening and understanding. Learn the art of listening by closing your mouth and focusing your mind on what's being said to you.

Practice listening to what is being said, how it's being said, and the non-verbal messages of facial expressions and body movement.

The Mentor's Self-Assessment

The purpose of this assessment is to make you think deeply and reflect on important matters that pertain to you. Often times, we overlook the treasures of insight, experience, and knowledge we possess, and thus never realize just how wealthy we are. When one discovers he is wealthy, he then becomes very willing to give away that wealth to others. It would be easy to read over this section and not to do it, but do not miss out on the value this exercise can bring to your soul.

There are ten questions in this assessment, and I want to coach you on a practical way to proceed. Answer only two questions per day, which means this will be completed in five days. Take one hour with each question and follow this sequence: READ the question to yourself; REPEAT it over in your mind; ASK God to give you insight, bring things to your remembrance, and give you clarity; and finally, WRITE down your answers.

Once these questions have been completed, talk to your spouse, a friend, or someone in your small group about your answers. Allow this person(s) to ask questions or challenge your answers if they are not biblically or morally sound. This will refine you and your answers. All clear? Okay mentors, prepare to begin tomorrow.

DAY 1

1. **What is your personal life vision or mission?** A vision is the big, mental picture for your future of who you will become and what you will do. It may start off broad, but the more you pray, think, read and talk about it, the clearer it will become. Write down the five major goals of your life. Then, form these into a paragraph, then into a few sentences.

    a. _____

      _____

    b. _____

      _____

    c. _____

      _____

    d. _____

      _____

    e. _____

      _____

2. <u>**What are your 5 core values that your decisions and behaviors are founded upon?**</u> Values are the things that are important to you to live out. They reside deep within you and were a part of your upbringing, education, and intentional development. One of my core values is faithfulness or consistency. To be present, to do what I am supposed to do, to hang in there and not quit is who I am. Think: what is important to you? Write down the five words or phrases that describe your answer.

a. _____
   _____

b. _____
   _____

c. _____
   _____

d. _____
   _____

e. _____
   _____

DAY 2

3. **What are your God-given gifts or talents that you and others have observed?** Every gift that you possess came from God. A gift is often times something that you naturally do well. It is an ability that was not obtained through education, but can be enhanced by education. It is innate within you and helps others; it solves problems and attracts people to you. Each of us know people who barely study and get all A's, never lift weights but are stronger than those who do, can connect with people instantly and effortlessly—these are gifts. Think about it. Ask others who know you and are around you. Write them down.

a. _____
   _____

b. _____
   _____

c. _____
   _____

d. _____
   _____

e. _____
   _____

4. **What 3 areas of social justice are you most passionate about bringing change to and why?** Social justice refers to the ills and moral choices that affect the well-being and protection of people in our society, especially vulnerable people like orphans, the homeless, the fatherless, and victims of human trafficking. Write down the ones that have lit a fire in your heart.

a. _____
   _____

b. _____
   _____

c. _____
   _____

DAY 3

5. <u>**What line of work has personally given you the most fulfillment? Why?**</u>

    a. _____

        _____

    b. _____

        _____

    c. _____

        _____

    d. _____

        _____

6. <u>**What are 3-5 skills you have learned (in school or by experience) and applied in work and relationships?**</u>
A skill is something you perform well because you have practiced. Another definition from the Merriam-Webster Dictionary is the "ability to use one's knowledge effectively and readily in execution or performance." A skill I've learned through working is conflict resolution. I don't recall learning this in college, but it has been and will continue to be invaluable. Write down your skills.

a. _____
_____

b. _____
_____

c. _____
_____

d. _____
_____

e. _____
_____

DAY 4

7. <u>**What are the 10 most important lessons you've learned thus far in life?**</u>

    a. _____

    _____

    b. _____

    _____

    c. _____

    _____

    d. _____

    _____

    e. _____

    _____

    f. _____

    _____

    g. _____

    _____

    h _____

    _____

    i. _____

    _____

    j. _____

    _____

8. **<u>What has God taught you about Himself?</u>** (i.e. He's forgiving, a provider etc.) God reveals Himself to us individually based on His nature and character, which is revealed in His Word. It seems that a crisis or problem sets the stage for God to reveal who He is in that moment or time. I think it's because when we're in need and desperate, we become more open. When we're weak, He reveals His strength. When we were discouraged, He's the lifter of our head. Go ahead and write what you've learned.

a. _____

_____

b. _____

_____

c. _____

_____

d. _____

_____

DAY 5

9. <u>**What have been your greatest challenges or troubles in life and how have you overcome them?**</u> All of us have gone through tough times where we're hurt, over-whelmed, and exasperated. Our focus during those times was to simply survive, and make it through. What we often neglect to do is pause, catch our breath, thank God for His help, and reflect on the lessons—what we did wrong, what we may have done right. God says in Isaiah 45:3 (NLT), "I will give you treasures hidden in darkness—secret riches." There is a saying that even in hard times, He's enriching us. Think about those treasures that helped you overcome and write them down.

a. _____

_____

b _____

_____

c. _____

_____

d. _____

_____

e. _____

_____

10. **<u>What do you want your legacy for God and this world</u> <u>to be before you die?</u>** Each of us will leave a legacy of some sort. I believe we all want it to be significant. This won't happen passively, but intentionally. What do you want to leave to your children, grandchildren, and great-grand-children? Write it down.

a. _____

_____

b. _____

_____

c. _____

_____

d. _____

_____

e. _____

_____

Thank you for taking the time to reflect, process, and write down your answers to these questions. By completing this assessment, you were able to discover, or re-discover, some meaningful information about yourself. The great truth to remember is God is not done with you. Your story continues to be written on this journey with Jesus. Just as He came and invited you along with Him, your goal should be to take someone along with you. You have knowledge, wisdom, and experience with God and in life that you can teach someone else. Taking someone with you is a natural part of life that includes practical steps—there's nothing lofty about this process.

Remember, show an interest in other people. This will pique their interest in wanting to connect with you. Next, develop a relationship with the person. As you are building the relationship, find moments to share what you know. Teachable moments can happen at any time, so take advantage of them. Most importantly, be willing to invest time. It takes an average of two years to get to know a young person, but the average mentor gives up after eighteen months. Your persistence and patience will enable you to share the knowledge, wisdom, and experience you've gained to enrich other lives.

Reflection Questions

1. Knowing we are all mentoring as we go through life, how has your life touched others?

2. As a mentor, how can you see yourself the way God sees you?

3. What thoughts do you have about yourself that are not God's thoughts about you?

4. How can you address wrong thinking in you, as well as your mentee?

My Prayer...

Lord, work in me an unshakeable confidence and peace as You use me to guide others.

Key No. 4

The Relationship, Role, and Responsibilities of a Mentor

Relationship is the pipeline by which truth comes through. It carries the waters of life, wisdom, and advice to the mentee. As a mentor, it's imperative for you to understand that relationship is the foundation of the mentor-mentee dynamic. If there is no relationship, it is like building a brick house with no mortar—nothing will stick and the structure will topple over. When there is no relationship, mentoring becomes just another impersonal way to receive information. It can be reduced to a process that comes across as cold, clinical, and religious because there is no connection. A good relationship is imperative for any true success to happen. Because mentoring is a relationship, it is right to assume that the relational dynamic will take time. In real estate, the top three words are: location, location, location. When it comes to mentoring, the top three words are relate, relate, relate.

God created us as social beings." And the Lord God said, "It is not good that man should be alone; I will make him a helper comparable to him" (Gen. 2:18). In the beginning of time, God created a helper for Adam. A mentor is essentially a helper—one who complements another to reach a goal. Ecclesiastes 4:9 says, "Two are better than one, because they have a good reward for their labor." In fact, the gospels show how Jesus sent His disciples out two by two to accomplish the work He established for them. At the end of the day, this truth stands clear: our hearts crave intimacy, familiarity, and friendship. We all want to know and be known.

Mentoring is built into the design of mankind because God created us to give and receive. The heart of a true mentor is to impart. "For I long to see you, that I may impart to you some spiritual gift, so that you may be established" (Rom. 1:11). Impart means to share, distribute, and grant—it implies a generosity or liberality on the part of the one sharing. A mentor's desire is to deposit good things into another. There are a number of things mentors deposit.

> *Mentoring is built into the design of mankind because God created us to give and receive*

The first is **information**. As a mentor, you want to fill in the blind spots of your mentee and supply what they don't know so they can be better informed about who they are and where they are headed.

Secondly, you want to deposit **understanding**. This is where you clarify what the mentee knows. You want to fine-tune the knowledge they currently possess.

Next is **wisdom**, and this is the process of the mentee applying the knowledge they have gained. They need to know how to use all of the information they received. It's no good if it's just stored up—they have to know how to walk it out.

Finally, you want to provide **inspiration**. Your goal is to motivate your mentee to act and keep on acting on what they know. Part of inspiration is instructing them on wrong information, so they can start using the right information. This will provide clarity and fuel them to move in the right direction with the right motives.

Responsibilities of the Mentor

Jesus is the Supreme Mentor; He expresses and models that we are to mentor with the goal of the mentee exceeding us. John 14:12 captures the essence of this. "Most assuredly, I say to you, he who believes in Me, the works that I do he will do also; and greater works than these he will do, because I go to My Father." Mentoring is designed so your mentee can accomplish greater impact and influence than yourself. Don't let this intimidate you or make you feel less than. A mentor wants the mentee to match him and then eventually surpass him. This is the mark of a true mentor—the ability to push your mentee to greater heights than you've ever known.

The ultimate role and responsibility of a mentor is to help the mentee grow. The roles and responsibilities go hand in hand. They are:

- Pray
- Be an example

- Care
- Advise/Counsel
- Show consistent character
- Teach/challenge
- Listen and ask questions
- Help with accountability
- Observe and address negative patterns

Speaking Words of Affirmation

You should routinely affirm your mentee and the vision and goals they are aiming for. A negative attitude and discouraging words do not foster motivation. As part of your affirmation process, you want to create regular feedback of your mentee and how they are growing and advancing—or not. Your feedback needs to happen on a regular basis and be honest in critique. Recognition is important as well. When you see your mentee conquer a fear or reach an accomplishment, celebrate the progress with him.

In his book, *Whale Done: The Power of Positive Relationships*, actor Ken Blanchard chronicles the story of rough-edged businessman, husband, and father, Wes Kingsley. Kingsley had visited SeaWorld, where he was amazed at the ability of the trainers to lead huge killer whales in performing acrobatic hurdles and dives. When he got the opportunity to chat with the chief trainer, he discovered the trainers' techniques of building trust, highlighting the positive, and redirecting negative behavior—which made those entertaining performances possible. Kingsley was forced to take a long, hard look at his own finger-pointing management style and come face to face with his faults as a manager and husband, which had created relationships void of trust. He began to see the difference between "GOTcha" (catching people doing things wrong) and "Whale Done!" (catching people doing things right). As a mentor, you create a safe and trustworthy environment. You want your mentee to rest in the fact that you have their best interest at heart.

Unlocking Potential

It can be easy to think of a mentor as a cheerleader of sorts, who sits on the sidelines and encourages the mentee as they work their way through obstacles en route to their goals. But a mentor is so much more than that. You have to see yourself as a miner of gold. You want the person you're mentoring to realize the treasure they possess. It's your goal to point them to the untapped strength that lies inside of them.

Mentoring is built into the design of mankind because God created us to give and receive

In the book *Deep Survival: Who Lives, Who Dies, and Why*, author Laurence Gonzales writes, "on Mother's Day 1999, Saint John Eberle and his partner, Marc Beverly, were climbing in New Mexico's Sandia Mountain Wilderness when a rock weighing more than 500 pounds fell on Eberle, pinning him. Beverly watched as Eberle lifted the rock off of himself." Gonzales recounted the story from an annual summary entitled "Accidents in North American Mountaineering." An article in the *Journal of Applied Physiology* (1961) titled "Some Factors Modifying the Expression of Human Strength," the authors Michio Ikaí and Arthur H. Steinhaus suggest the following: that one's inability to exert oneself to the physiological maximum is the result of "acquired inhibitions that in turn are subject to disinhibition by pure Pavlovian procedures, by anesthetization of inhibitory mechanisms, or by pharmacologically induced symptoms serving as stimuli for disinhibition."

Now, let me simplify all of that: you are always capable of great physical feats, but it takes a crisis for you to actually perform them. As a mentor, you can play a huge role as a motivator in encouraging another to pull that extraordinary, untapped strength to the surface. Potential is always waiting to happen. It's already lying within you; it simply needs a critical point in life or an unusual predicament to be displayed.

Simply put, there is more to your mentee than meets the eye. Take for example Mrs. Dougherty, a retired Chicago public school teacher whose experience is well-known in the education arena. One year, the highly-regarded sixth grade teacher was faced with a class she had trouble controlling. She concluded that many of them must have serious learning disabilities. While the principal was out, she did something forbidden—she looked into a special file that listed the student's IQs. She was astonished to discover that most of her students' intelligence was well above average, with IQs in the 120s and 130s. Turns out one of the worst students had an IQ of 145.

Upset that she had been giving the students remedial work and setting low expectations for them, Mrs. Dougherty increased the homework, assigned more challenging work, and laid down strict consequences for misbehavior. Slowly but surely, the students' performance improved. By the end of the year, the problem student was the best behaved and received the best grades.

The principal was pleased with the reversal and asked Mrs. Dougherty what caused the change. She confessed the truth. He forgave her and acknowledged the effort she'd made in making a change. He then said, "I think you should know, Mrs. Dougherty, those numbers next to the children's names—those are not their IQ scores. Those are their locker numbers."[3]

When potential is kept, it self-destructs. This is what was happening in those early days of Mrs. Dougherty's class. She had not yet tapped into her student's potential, so neither she nor they knew what they could accomplish. Potential is capable of being, but not yet in existence. Potential is latent power that has not been unleashed yet. God has created everyone with potential. But you and your mentee will never be happy or fulfilled if the capacity for growth is never developed. God grants each person with potential—not just for personal gain, but for the benefit of others. Ask God to show you the keys to release potential within those whom you mentor. What crisis or challenge will become the catalyst in unlocking potential?

---

[3] Carl Boyd, "No One Rises to Low Expectations," a conference address given at *"Hear Their Cries: A Faith Community Response to Child Abuse"* at the University of Missouri – Kansas City, May 10, 1995

Mentoring Others in Spiritual Disciplines

Part of your responsibility as a mentor is to teach. As a Christian mentor, instilling spiritual disciplines in your mentee should be a top priority.

> Train yourself for godliness; for while bodily training is of some value, godliness is of value in every way, as it holds promise for the present life and also for the life to come. (1 Timothy 4:7-8 ESV)

Spiritual disciplines help to train us for our walk with God and help to make our faith strong and healthy. Any good sports coach makes sure to take their team through rigorous practice, so when they go out on the field they are prepared for the game. This same premise applies with spiritual disciplines. As mentor, you are like a spiritual coach helping your mentee to be fit for the purpose God has called them to fulfill.

Reading is a foundational, daily practice in the life of a Christian. It's how we learn the narrative of Scripture, which transforms our thinking and nourishes our faith. It was the custom of Jesus to read the Scriptures (Luke 4:16-17), and it should be ours, too. Begin reading in the gospel of John and continue through the book of Revelation. Then, begin at Matthew and read through to the end again. Schedule 15 minutes a day of unhurried time with your Bible—you'll be glad you did.

Biblical meditation is the mental activity of focused and repetitive musing on a biblical truth. This normally comes about through something that you've read that stands out to you. What do you do? You highlight and give more thought to the word, phrase, or story that's captured your attention.

This spiritual discipline includes muttering to oneself what you've been thinking on. God promises if we practice consistently meditating on His Word day and night, we'll make our way prosperous and successful (Josh. 1:8; Ps. 1:2-3). A suggested time to begin this practice is three to five minutes.

Studying the Bible is the next spiritual discipline to activate that will take you further on a specific topic, person, or story in the Bible. Studying means you will have a topic in mind (i.e. servanthood, anger, parenting, etc.), have your computer (or pad and pen), and you'll begin to search a word or phrase and look up all references. You might even purchase a Vine's Expository Dictionary or a Bible study app. Studying the Bible may not be something you practice daily like reading, but when you do, schedule one hour to really dig and search.

Prayer – Like reading the Bible, prayer is a spiritual exercise we should practice daily. The importance of prayer was modeled and taught by Jesus, but the significance of it in one's life was revealed in the question posed by Christ's disciples. "Lord, teach us to pray, as John also taught his disciples" (Luke 11:1). The disciples could've desired to learn how to teach, preach, heal, cast out demons, or work miracles, but they didn't. I surmise that the disciples recognized that the powers Jesus possessed to do all the above were byproducts of prayer.

Worship – Worship is about drawing near to God from your heart. It's you and I approaching and acknowledging who God says He is in His Word. This is worshipping Him "in truth" as Jesus taught in John 4. Worship can be done at anytime and anywhere, but I would recommend it be included as an aspect of our prayer time.

Waiting on the Lord – This phrase carries several different biblical definitions. Habakkuk 2:1 provides us with a picture of a man waiting to hear what God will speak to Him. This means that we have more than likely been speaking to God in prayer, but now we've quieted our hearts and minds for the purpose of listening to His still, small voice.

This spiritual discipline completes the "listening side" of our dialogue with God. I am not saying every time you and I wait we're guaranteed God will speak. What I am saying is waiting gives God the opportunity to speak to our hearts. As a result, our hearts become more sensitive and receptive to His voice.

Confession – God has given us a way to live right before Him through confession. It simply means telling God that we were wrong based on our understanding of His Word. God says lying is wrong, so if we tell a lie we can admit this mistake to God and He will forgive and cleanse us (I John 1:9). This is the most common foundational application of confession, but here are a few more.

Once you've confessed your sin to God, there is still a need to confess to another trusted friend. This person can pray for the repetition and pain of this sin to be broken so you can be healed (James 5:16).

This fast application of confession is to say what God says about Himself, who He says we are, what He's given us, and more. Here are some examples of this:

- God is good and faithful.
- I'm trusting God for my future.
- The Lord is my Healer.
- I'm an overcomer through Christ.

Qualities of a Mentor

Being a mentor is something anyone with a heart to engage can actually do. Spotless perfection is not required, but there are some qualities that will make you effective in helping those whom you mentor to grow and develop. Some of these qualities have been made clearer for you through what you answered in your assessment, but these are worth mentioning again.

Character: As a mentor, you want to have character, not be one. At the root of character is your integrity. Integrity has to do with honesty with yourself and being truthful in how you deal with others. Character is keeping your word, not misrepresenting yourself to get others to like you. When you have integrity, it gives you credibility and creates confidence. The Great Wall of China is a series of fortification systems built across the northern borders of China in the seventeenth century to protect Chinese states and empires against invaders. Even after it was completed, it suffered three invasions. Why would this happen after such careful and deliberate planning? Because the gatekeeper was bribed to let the enemy in. The gatekeeper lacked character and integrity, which resulted in a weakened defense for China.

Clear vision: We are not talking visual sight through the eye, but rather of mental sight—a dream or a goal. Clear vision provides the purpose of your mentoring relationship. It establishes direction and points the way for where you are to lead your mentee. If you don't have a vision for your mentoring relationships, you can easily veer off course with your mentee. Write the vision down and review it regularly.

Passion: Passion is the wood in the fire, the fuel in the car, and it's the way the bull feels when he sees red. Passion gives you a zeal and enthusiasm for what you do. Without it, you will likely burn out in the mentoring relationship.

A desire to serve: The greatest display of mentoring is service. You must be willing to do first what you ask and expect of others. Vision is at the head of leadership, but at the heart of leadership is service. There was a college student in the Philippines who was upset over the filthy and neglected condition of the men's bathroom. He complained to the principal, who took care of the matter. The student was happy to see the problem being corrected, but was amazed that it was the principal himself who was doing the cleaning. That is the kind of heart we have as mentors.

Accessibility: This is an important quality of a mentor. Accessibility is being in a place where you can be touched and spoken to. It's hard to build a relationship with someone whom you don't have access to. Stay in a position to listen and be available.

Reflection Questions

1. How can you identify the needs of your mentee so you can better equip them in their life?

2. How do you expose or reveal blind spots so they can be set free?

3. How would you gently and constructively address a negative behavior pattern?

4. What are tangible ways that you can discover the treasures within your mentee?

5. What spiritual disciplines could you practice with your mentee?

My Prayer...

Father, help me to be patient while instilling truth into the lives You entrust to me.

Key No. 5

Four Ways to Unlock Your Mentee's Potential

As human beings, we often fail to see the good or the potential within ourselves that others may see. Instead, we are acutely aware of our own shortcomings, and much of our mental and emotional focus is on trying to improve these perceived flaws. This perspective creates blinders that impair us from having clarity as it relates to our God-given potential. One of the great joys of being a mentor is helping your mentee understand the keys that will unleash their latent potential. The story of Gideon helps us understand a major key in the discovery and release of potential, which is embracing your identity in God.

In Judges 6, the children of Israel did evil in the sight of the Lord. So, the Lord delivered them into the hand of Midian for seven years. As a result, the Midianites ravished the Israelites' land, leaving nothing for them to eat.

> Now the Angel of the Lord came and sat under the terebinth tree which was in Ophrah, which belonged to Joash the Abiezrite, while his son Gideon threshed wheat in the winepress, in order to hide it from the Midianites. And the Angel of the Lord appeared to him, and said to him, "The Lord is with you, you mighty man of valor!" Gideon said to Him, "O my lord, if the Lord is with us, why then has all this happened to us? And where are all His miracles which our fathers told us about, saying, 'Did not the Lord bring us up from Egypt?' But now the Lord has forsaken us and delivered us into the hands of the Midianites." Then the Lord turned to him and said, "Go in this might of yours, and you shall save Israel from the hand of the Midianites. Have I not sent you? (Judges 6:11-14)

God called Gideon a "mighty man of valor" and told him to go in this might of his even though he was hiding from the Midianites. Gideon did not know it, but he was a mighty man of valor. He probably never heard this kind of description about himself before, but he heard it from God. The Lord knows how He has fashioned us individually and what He has placed on the inside of us. So, in His Word we discover who we are, and, if we believe it, the way we think and the way we see ourselves will change.

In addition to believing what God says about us, there are other catalysts that will unlock and unleash the potential that exists in a mentee including: crisis, cause, compassion, and collaboration.

Let's begin with **crisis**. A crisis can reveal the latent power within us. A crisis can be defined as a time of intense difficulty or danger, or a time when a difficult or important decision must be made. In life, your mentees will experience these crisis moments more than just a few times. As a mentor, you can help your mentees gain a proper perspective on these moments of crisis as opposed to viewing them from a negative perspective. The right perspective enables your mentee to understand that the crisis will draw out their strength and conviction by clarifying what they believe and stand for.

There is an example of this in the Bible involving a young teenage girl named Esther. A man named Haman, who was a high-ranking official of the King, hatched a plan to annihilate the Jewish people because Mordecai (Esther's uncle) would not bow to him, or pay him homage. In the hottest part of this conflict, Esther rose to her potential even at the risk of her own life and revealed Haman's plot to wipe out the Jewish people. She even stated "If I perish, I perish!" Wow! Where did this kind of conviction come from? Did it appear suddenly? No. It had always been inside of Esther, but this particular crisis drew it out of her.

Help your mentee see that they already possess what it takes in those moments of crisis to make right choices and do the right thing.

The second catalyst that will unlock and release potential is a **cause**. There are many causes in the world that people are passionate about. Your mentee will more than likely be passionate about a few causes based on how they are wired and what they deem important. A cause will lead your mentee to discover their capacity—the ability to understand and use information to make proper decisions, then communicate those decisions. This can launch a mentee into new accomplishments. It might be organizing a team to serve at a community event, or feeding the homeless; it might be literacy for children and adults, or justice for those who cannot afford legal expenses. The list goes on and on.

There was a day when a young Jewish boy named David went to take supplies to the war where his brothers were enlisted as soldiers at the request of their father, Jesse. As David approached on this fateful day, he heard a Philistine giant named Goliath spewing verbal assaults against the armies of Israel. Upon hearing these words of Goliath, David was moved to ask two questions: "who is this uncircumcised Philistine that he should defy the armies of the living God?" and "Is there not a cause?"

David went out to fight Goliath in the Valley of Elah with nothing more than his slingshot and a pouch of smooth stones. Goliath was bigger than David, had more experience in war than David, and had larger weapons than David, but David had a cause that was eternally larger than Goliath: "that all the earth may know that there is a God in Israel."

Have you ever heard of Anjezë Gonxhe Bojaxhiu? This is the name of the late Mother Teresa, who had a cause of caring for the poor and sick on the streets of Calcutta, India. This cause became her life's work and catapulted her into national prominence. Helping your mentee locate their cause in life will unlock passion and purpose.

A third catalyst that can propel your mentee into their potential is **compassion**. Matthew 14:13-14 says, "When Jesus heard it, he departed from there by boat to a deserted place by himself. But when the multitudes heard it, they followed him on foot from the cities. And when Jesus went out he saw a great multitude; and he was moved with compassion for them, and healed their sick."

Jesus had just heard that his cousin, John the Baptist, had been beheaded, and this was horrible news. Jesus was one-hundred percent God, but was also one-hundred percent man. Thus, He sought a quiet place to retreat and grieve over John's demise; but something happened when He saw the crowd. He looked at them and realized they were like sheep with no shepherd—no direction and no protection. Amongst them were many who were sick and suffering, and, despite His own personal grief over His cousin's death, something within Jesus compelled Him to go and heal those who were sick. It was compassion. There are times when we all feel sympathy for the plight of other people who are suffering. This is natural, but sympathy is not compassion. The difference is that compassion moves you into action. This inward compulsion causes one to not think primarily of himself, but of others. Whenever Jesus was moved with compassion, miracles always followed. As a wise mentor, you can help your mentee become aware of the power and potential of the compassion of God within them.

The final catalyst in helping your mentee unlock his or her potential is **collaboration**. No matter how great one's potential may be, it will never be fully realized without the help of others. Collaboration is defined as the action of working with someone to produce or create something. Collaboration will stir up creativity, challenge ideas and make one search to think more deeply. It creates an environment where there is an accountability to produce. Let's consider the parable of the talents in Matthew 25:14-17:

> For the kingdom of heaven is like a man traveling to a far country, who called his own servants and delivered his goods to them. And to one he gave five talents, to another two, and to another one, to each according to his own ability; and immediately he went on a journey. Then he who had received the five talents went and traded with them, and made another five talents. And likewise he who had received two gained two more also.

The word "traded" means to work, be active, or accomplish something. The potential within a mentee cannot be developed in isolation, but will be developed and deployed in collaborative settings. Thus, encourage your mentee to get involved in working with others, even those who might be different than them. Working with different people causes one to develop more fully as opposed to only working with like-minded individuals.

I was challenged by a friend of mine to write a song, and my response to him was "I don't write songs, I'm a preacher." Then I heard the Holy Spirit remind me of Philippians 4:13, which says, "I can do all things through Christ who strengthens me." So, I went to the studio in Hollywood to lay down some vocals and it was a tremendous experience. But one of the things I was most enamored about was watching the creative and collaborative process of the creation of melodies and lyrics for amazing songs. It was like watching different sections of an orchestra begin to play their instruments and parts to create a beautiful, harmonic blend of music

Once you discover potential, it's imperative to speak to and about the potential of your mentee. Your words have incredible power to nurture limitless possibilities. Pablo Picasso said, "My mother said to me, if you become a soldier, you'll be a general; if you become a monk, you'll end up as Pope. Instead I became a painter and wound up Picasso." Don't hold back in speaking to the potential of your mentee. Be generous with your encouragement in regard to what you see in them, even in its earliest forms—gifts, talents, strengths, and positives about their personality.

Through the process of discovery and development of potential, you must remember to point your mentee to God, who is the source of life and the giver of their potential, because without Him we could do nothing. Let the release of power and potential always bring honor and glory to God.

Reflection Questions

1. How can you help your mentee during a crisis to see God's hand at work?

2. As a mentor, what can you do to cultivate potential?

3. What are practical ways you can support your mentee in what they are passionate about?

4. For you and your mentee, what situation(s) mentioned in this chapter predominantly reveal your strengths through either crisis, for a cause, through compassion, or with collaboration?

5. Once potential is realized, how can you develop it to have maximum impact?

My Prayer...

Lord, help me to see my mentees through Your eyes and speak Your words to encourage their potential.

Key No. 6

The Steps to Mentoring

When it comes to the practice of mentoring, there are several examples that provide clear illustrations on how to proceed. The one who will be our model on how mentoring works is none other than Elijah, along with his younger counterpart, Elisha. In 1 Kings 19, we learn that Elijah was a prophet in Israel with a miracle ministry. He was devoted to God and loved the nation of Israel. God's people had moved away from Him because King Ahab and his wife Jezebel worshiped Baal, the most popular Canaanite deity, whom they believe brought the rain and plentiful harvest. Elijah confronted Ahab and prophesied that there would be no dew or rain except at Elijah's word—as a result, it didn't rain for three years and six months. God supernaturally provided, protected and gave Elijah power the entire time, but this wasn't the end of God's miraculous work through Elijah. The prophet told Ahab to gather all Israel, the 450 prophets of Baal as well as the 400 prophets of Asherah.

While gathered on Mount Carmel, Elijah repaired the altar with twelve stones. He then dug a trench around the altar, arranged wood in the trench, and laid cut-up oxen up onto the wood. Next, he commanded water be poured three times over the offering until it filled the trench. Then, Elijah prayed to God and fire fell from heaven and consumed the water. The entire nation responded by falling on their faces, and crying out, "The Lord, He is God! The Lord, He is God!" Elijah ordered the 450 prophets of Baal to be killed with the sword, but because the nation turned to God after this, Elijah went to the top of Mount Carmel and prayed for rain for them. As the sky became black with clouds and a heavy rain fell, the hand of the Lord came upon Elijah allowing him to outrun King Ahab's chariot (a six-mile trip) to Jezreel.

Just twenty-four hours after being used to turn the nation of Israel back to God, Elijah received word that Jezebel was going to kill him. Such fear rose up in him that he ran to Beersheba through Judah and sat under a juniper tree and prayed to die. This was a result of emotional, mental, and physical exhaustion, as well as working alone. Lewis Clarke once said, "I have lived long enough! I can do no good among these people, let me now end my days." This pretty much sums up the mindset of Elijah. Fresh off a triumph, he suddenly felt like a failure. How did he get to that place?

He was alone—with no one to encourage him or to talk to and simply be his friend. He lamented the lack of success of his fathers, the lack of success in turning the king to God, and running from the problem after just being full of faith and seeing God move only exacerbated his dismal state.

But in His kindness, God reached out to this depressed prophet. He let Elijah rest, provided food and drink, and gave him practical advice that many of us need today in time of trouble—lay down, rest, eat, and drink. Sometimes the answer to your anguish is to eat a good meal then go to bed.

> And there he went into a cave, and spent the night in that place; and behold, the word of the Lord came to him, and He said to him, "What are you doing here, Elijah?" So he said, "I have been very zealous for the Lord God of hosts; for the children of Israel have forsaken Your covenant, torn down Your altars, and killed Your prophets with the sword. I alone am left; and they seek to take my life. (1 Kings 19:9-14)

Now Elijah was ready to receive a fresh revelation and new instructions from God. As he stood on the mountain, God passed by in the wind, causing the rocks to break, but God was not in the rocks. Then there was an earthquake, but the Lord was not in the quake. Then a fire, but the Lord was not in the fire. Finally, there came a still, small voice—a gentle whisper. This is how God revealed Himself to Elijah, and He will do the same for you. Elijah was used to God performing miracles through his ministry, but God knew what Elijah needed was His still, small voice.

Perhaps you have felt like Elijah: despondent, depressed, a big failure. You wonder if you have made a difference, forgetting all that God's done for you, in you, and through you. The enemy has lied to you and told you to quit and give up, but don't do it. God says, "You are not a failure." He does not want you to forget the good work you've done with Him. So don't carry the problems of the world on your shoulders—that's God's role. He has more for you to do!

God's purpose for you is to raise up a generation of influencers by mentoring them.

> Then the Lord said to him: "Go, return on your way to the Wilderness of Damascus; and when you arrive, anoint Hazael as king over Syria. Also you shall anoint Jehu the son of Nimshi as king over Israel. And Elisha the son of Shaphat of Abel Meholah you shall anoint as prophet in your place. It shall be that whoever escapes the sword of Hazael, Jehu will kill; and whoever escapes the sword of Jehu, Elisha will kill. Yet I have reserved seven thousand in Israel, all whose knees have not bowed to Baal, and every mouth that has not kissed him." (1 Kings 19:15-18)

In this passage, God wanted to raise up Hazael, a Gentile king, Jehu to be king of Israel, and Elisha as a successor to Elijah. Elijah had complained because the past generation failed and the present generation hadn't done any better. Now God called him to help equip the future generation by anointing two kings and a prophet. It's interesting how God was going to use Elijah to do something to effect change in the future. By the time Elisha and Jehu completed their work, Baal worship was almost wiped out in Israel (2 Kings 10:18-31). No one generation can do everything, but each generation must see to it that the following generations are trained and that the tools are made available for them to continue the work of the Lord. God would use the swords of Hazael and Jehu and the words and works of Elisha to accomplish His purposes in the land. Even more, He assured Elijah that his own ministry hadn't been a failure, for there were still 7,000 people in the land who were faithful to Jehovah. The Lord didn't gather all 7,000 people together in a mass meeting. This was not His strategy at this time. Now, don't get me wrong, there's a place for sermons and large meetings, but we must never underestimate the importance of working with individuals.

Of these three leaders Elijah was tasked to anoint, there is one example that provides the clearest picture of what God is saying to us today. This is the relationship between Elijah and Elisha, his successor as a prophet in Israel. In this relationship, we learn what God is calling us to do in this hour, and that is mentoring. The dynamic between Elijah and Elisha provides practical lessons for us to absorb and apply.

The first lesson is to embrace mentoring as your calling. Each of us has a unique and specific calling from God to fulfill. If you are called to media, writing, working with children, singing, professional sports, acting, civil service, or business, mentoring is still your calling. We often don't realize it at first because we're focused on the discovering and doing part of our calling, but there's a duplication gene in every calling from God. Just as a coin has two sides, the other side of your calling is mentoring. The Scriptures show that mentoring was a vital part of Elijah's calling. It was a vital part of Moses's calling as he passed the mantle to Joshua and Caleb. It was a vital part of Paul's calling as he took Timothy and Titus under his wing.

And it was a central aspect of Jesus's calling, as seen in His commission to the church in Matthew 28:19-20: "Go therefore and make disciples of all the nations, baptizing them in the name of the Father and of the Son and of the Holy Spirit, teaching them to observe all things that I have commanded you; and lo, I am with you always, even to the end of the age."

The second lesson is to find connection. As you begin to embrace this truth, you can help others get to a place in life that has been designed for them by God. I believe many adults have unconsciously tapped into this innate quality of our God-given DNA. This is why one-on-one mentoring relationships with young people have increased from 500,000 in 2002 to approximately 3 million according to www. nationalservice.gov. Yet, the need for more mentors exists, so it's time to answer your call. You must embrace this aspect of your calling so you can teach others in a shorter time period than what may have taken you years to learn. If you do, then the next generation can take the church into a greater place of influence around the globe. Elijah initiated connection with Elisha, as seen in 1 Kings 19:19-21:

> So he departed from there, and found Elisha the son
> of Shaphat, who was plowing with twelve yoke of oxen
> before him, and he was with the twelfth. Then Elijah
> passed by him and threw his mantle on him. And he
> left the oxen and ran after Elijah, and said, "Please let
> me kiss my father and my mother, and then I will follow
> you." And he said to him, "Go back again, for what have
> I done to you?" So Elisha turned back from him, and
> took a yoke of oxen and slaughtered them and boiled

their flesh, using the oxen's equipment, and gave it to the people, and they ate. Then he arose and followed Elijah, and became his servant.

God may put someone on your heart and you can't stop thinking about them. He may lead you to someone or cause you to be naturally drawn to a person. This happened when I was playing basketball at PCH in Long Beach. I was somehow highlighted to Cardale. He saw something in me, so he made an effort and spent time with me. The connection may not be clear at first, because you may not be picking up why God is bringing attention to a person. Think of when you have a bad connection on your cell phone. Sometimes you have to adjust your position until the connection is clear. The same is true with mentoring. There may be times when the connection with another person seems weak or it drops and then returns. You will have to use wisdom in adjusting yourself to help the connection work.

Once you've established a connection, the key component is care. The late writer Maya Angelou shared this knowledge: "In order to be a mentor, and an effective one, one must care." The truth is, you do not have to be an expert, a genius, or a highly educated or charismatic person. You can simply know what you know, while at the same time showing a person you care about them. Bottom line, no one cares how much you know until they know how much you care.

The third lesson in mentoring is to clarify the purpose. Elisha knew what it meant when the mantle was placed upon him. He was going to be Elijah's successor as the next prophet to Israel. This was as clear as if he had actually said, "This means you're my replacement." Jesus clarified the mentoring purpose with His disciples by saying, "Come follow Me and I will make you fishers of men." He was clear in communicating His intention with the disciples. Mentoring will be more effective and efficient when the mentor and mentee have a mutual understanding of the purpose.

I had the privilege of mentoring some young leaders in my home church for the purpose of communicating the Word through preaching and teaching. We spent a year and a half discussing the foundational prerequisites of speaking, details of sermon preparation, how to deliver a message from the stage, as well as other aspects of the process. All involved knew the purpose of our meeting and there was no confusion as to why they were present.

A significant component of clarifying purpose is to determine your mentee's desires and needs from their relationship with you. What do they need to know? What area(s) do they want to grow in? Do they need to learn how to pray? How to better manage their time? How to balance work and relationships? Help with understanding their purpose? Once you establish what the purpose is, you can then be clear on what your expectations are, such as how often you will be getting together, at what time, and for how long. I have been in mentoring scenarios where the mentees are unsure of what they need; the only thing that is clear is there is an aching void in their life, and they see having a mentor as the answer. Sometimes it's good for your mentee to be around a solid Christian man or woman whom they can trust. Even if this is the case, be sure to define and articulate this as the purpose.

This is vital, because a lack of clarity can lead to disappointment and disillusionment; be diligent in clearly defining the parameters of the relationship, as well as the expectations.

The fourth lesson we can learn from Elijah and Elisha is mentoring is a commitment to serve. "So Elisha turned back from him, and took a yoke of oxen and slaughtered them and boiled their flesh, using the oxen's equipment, and gave it to the people, and they ate. Then he arose and followed Elijah, and became his servant" (1 Kings 19:21). Elisha was not burning a bridge between he and his family—rather, he was demonstrating his commitment to God, himself and Elijah. Consider this story from *Clever Magazine*:

> A friend was in front of me coming out of church one day, and the preacher was standing at the door as he always is to shake hands. He grabbed my friend by the hand and pulled him aside. The pastor said to him, "You need to join the army of the Lord!"
> My friend replied, "I'm already in the army of the Lord, pastor."
> The pastor questioned, "How come I don't see you except Christmas and Easter?"
> He whispered back, "I'm in the secret service."

The mentoring relationship cannot be built on a passive commitment. Dedication to the relationship is essential for both mentor and mentee in order for progressive development, which leads to greater fruitfulness and effectiveness. In 1 Kings 19:21, it says that Elisha became Elijah's servant. This position refers to one where tasks are performed by the closest servants of God, or a king, with a spirit of yielding and obedience. Egos cannot thrive in this situation. Mentoring is not about a position or title for self-promotion. It's a call to servanthood. Elisha served under Elijah for ten years. Elisha's claim to fame was that he was "the one who poured water on the hands of Elijah." In other words, servanthood was Elisha's chief characteristic. Isn't this why employers look for community service and volunteer participation on the resumés of potential hires? They're looking for the evidence of servanthood. He did not go down in the history books only for having prophesied more than his predecessor, nor for having performed more miracles, but being known for his heart to serve.

Elisha's ministry spanned more than fifty years and impacted four nations: Israel, Judah, Moab, and Syria. Because he yielded with such commitment to being a servant, it set him up to have a lasting, fruitful ministry. When it comes to mentoring, your commitment to be a servant will determine the depth, impact, and duration of your work. 2 Timothy 2:2 says, "And the things that you have heard from me among many witnesses, commit these to faithful (committed) men who will be able to teach others also." Committing is the act of placing alongside and to deposit as trust for protection. This is exactly what we see happening with Elijah and Elisha. Elijah deposited the good things God gave him into Elisha as he came alongside him, because he was faithful and trustworthy.

The fifth lesson is exhibiting character. Because of his high level of character, Elijah was qualified for the high office of prophet. His character also made him the right kind of mentor for Elisha. As a mentee (and future mentor), Elisha's character was demonstrated through his humility, patience, and honor.

Elisha's humility was seen as he served the man of God. The mark of a true servant is his humility.

> He has shown you, O man, what is good;
> And what does the Lord require of you
> But to do justly,
> To love mercy,
> And to walk humbly with your God? (Micah 6:8)

When Elijah was later separated from Elisha and went up to heaven in a chariot of fire (2 Kings 2), Elijah's mantle fell down to the ground. And before Elisha picked it up, he ripped his own clothes, which in the Bible symbolized humility and mourning.

Elisha also showed patience—another aspect of character. Elijah never talked about how long Elisha would have to serve him, and as far as we know, Elisha never asked. He didn't push for a promotion or jockey for position. He just attended to Elijah patiently. Elisha also showed great perseverance in learning to wait on God, for he never once said throughout his ten years of service those four words kids love to scream from the backseat on a road trip: "Are we there yet?" Elisha did not have what's called "destination disease." This is the mentality that is so focused on arriving that one misses the beauty and lessons of the journey. No, he just kept on serving, having no idea when his day would come. The only way I know to cultivate patience is to focus on God, and on what is in front of me right now.

Patience is essential because mentoring is about development and growth, which both take time. It is said that the Chinese bamboo tree begins as a nut— the size of a walnut. Once planted it must be watered and fertilized every day for the next five years. However, in the fifth year, it breaks through the ground and grows nine feet in six weeks. Mentoring requires watering and fertilizing; then growth will occur.

The only way I know to cultivate patience is to focus on God, and on what is in front of me right now

Another facet of character displayed in Elisha's life is honor. Elisha honored Elijah as his mentor. Elijah did not just see himself as Elisha's mentor, but as a father figure to the young future prophet. Deuteronomy 21 notes the inheritance of the first-born being a double portion; so when Elijah asked, "What shall I give you?" Elisha knew what to ask for in order to show honor to Elijah by treating the elder prophet as his father and asking for a double portion of the spirit Elijah had. This must have touched the prophet's heart, since he had no biological son.

When Elijah was carried to heaven, Elisha did not cry out, "Finally, it's about time!" Rather, he cried out, "My father, my father!" Elisha honored Elijah by putting on the mantle and then practicing what he had been taught by Elijah.

The final step in the mentoring process is to decide to conclude or continue the mentoring relationship.

When Elijah was taken up into heaven, that brought an end to the relationship with Elisha. When the mentoring relationship ends, it is time for the mentor to move on to the next thing God has for him or her. Of course, the conclusion of the mentoring should be mutually agreed upon. The mentee must continue to apply the training and knowledge received from mentoring in order to grow. While the mentoring may come to a close, the relationship should continue in the form of friendship and ongoing fellowship.

In an employment scenario, the mentoring relationship may have a set timeline, so the decision to conclude has already been made. Some churches or organizations may determine the mentoring timeline depending on the situation, person, or position. It could be three months, six months, nine months, a year, or more. Even when a mentoring relationship has officially concluded, the mentee should be given the "open door policy." This means they can always return to talk, ask questions, or even clear their head and heart through venting.

To summarize the lessons: Mentoring is part of your **Calling**, so seek and find **Connection** in order to pass on what you have to those around you. **Clarify** the purpose of the mentoring relationship. **Commit** to serving and developing **Character**. Lastly, choose to either **Conclude** or **Continue** the mentoring relationship.

Reflection Questions

1. What ways can you train and equip your mentee to eventually be a mentor?

2. As a mentor, how can you train and provide tools to those following you to continue the work of the Lord?

3. If you've lost connection with a mentee, how can you change or correct the relationship?

4. In Elijah's season of despair, he rested and ate. What are some steps you can take to encourage and refresh yourself in a similar season?

5. How can you connect to a potential mentee through a common purpose with a commitment to character development?

My Prayer...

Father, open my eyes to see mentoring as my calling and enable me to find connection with those I mentor.

Key No. 7

Discovering Mentoring Opportunities

When it comes to finding mentees, there is no shortage of places to discover them. A key component is creating opportunities in your life for a mentee to be discovered. Think about leaving days and times open for a mentee. Make yourself available by intentionally placing yourself in situations where you can connect with a potential mentee. This is not stalking, but being open and available to becoming a mentor. This could include eating in the workplace cafeteria so you can meet new people or staying after church, so you're available for conversations you wouldn't normally have. A mentee may also be someone you're assigned to already at work, in church, or in an organization you are part of. This is a bonus because there is already an infrastructure set up to facilitate reaching out and meeting.

Build a network of people with interests, passions, and goals that match yours, both online and offline—that way you create more opportunities for communication. As you observe and interact with others, this will give potential mentees a chance to observe you and vice versa. As mentor, you choose who to take under your wing, but the mentee also gets to choose if they'll take you up on the offer. It's a two-way street.

Practical Steps in Selecting a Mentee

The first step in finding a mentee is not a difficult one—all it takes is you being observant. Look around you and see who's there. More often than not, the person you are to mentor is someone you already know, or who is in your circle of influence—a son or daughter, a younger sibling, niece or nephew, a cousin, a new employee, a co-worker, or the kid who lives down the street from you. So, look around you and see who's there.

In Exodus 18:21, Jethro instructed Moses to select from all the people when it came time to find those who could help him and who he could impart knowledge to.

> Moreover you shall select from all the people able men, such as fear God, men of truth, hating covetousness; and place such over them to be rulers of thousands, rulers of hundreds, rulers of fifties, and rulers of tens.

The people Moses has been walking with and leading were those who were ripe for mentoring. This same principle is evident in the New Testament. In Acts 6:3, the apostles were told to "seek out from among you seven men of good reputation, full of the Holy Spirit and wisdom, whom we may appoint over this business." The main point from both of these passages is that the persons who were selected were already there.

Select someone whom God highlights. There is no shortage of ways God can communicate to you to spotlight a person. More often than not, God will call attention to a characteristic or quality in that person, such as a desire to know God or to be used by Him. You may notice they possess a teachable heart and attitude. Their penchant for taking on responsibility or accountability may be traits that draw you to them. Or they may have exhibited a similar gifting and calling as you.

Seek someone who is faithful or sincerely desires your help. In Mark chapter 10, a rich young ruler came to Jesus seeking His help. When he saw Jesus on the road, the rich young ruler came running, knelt before Jesus, and asked Him, "Good Teacher, what shall I do that I may inherit eternal life?"

So Jesus said to him, "Why do you call Me good? No one is good but One, that is, God. You know the commandments: 'Do not commit adultery,' 'Do not murder,' 'Do not steal,' 'Do not bear false witness,' 'Do not defraud,' 'Honor your father and your mother.' "

The rich young ruler answered, "Teacher, all these things I have kept from my youth."

Then Jesus said to him, "One thing you lack: Go your way, sell whatever you have and give to the poor, and you will have treasure in heaven; and come, take up the cross, and follow Me."

The account ends with, "But he was sad at this word, and went away sorrowful, for he had great possessions."

The ruler came seeking help, but when Jesus offered him the help he needed, he decided that wasn't really the help he was looking for. His heart was not sincere. If it was, he would have heeded the advice Jesus gave him instead of walking away sadly. As a mentor, you have to be able to discern if someone is honestly wanting your help.

One time I was hosting Wayne Meyers, a man whom God has used mightily in Mexico for over sixty years. I was his driver for the evening and wanted to make sure he was comfortable and had the space to get ready to speak to our Bible school students. I didn't say much on the drive, but distinctly remember him telling me, "Son, there are two kinds of people: those who need your help, and those who want to waste your time. You have to discern between the two." Not everyone will want your help as a mentor, and you can discern the ones who do.

Connecting Generationally

As we apply these steps to mentoring, there is yet another relational dynamic that we must be aware of, and that is our generational differences.

The Bible reveals that God works generationally. His plan is not to work exclusively with one or two generations, but with all. He is the God of Abraham, Isaac, and Jacob. We cultivate relationships with the generations that follow us in order to pass on eternal truth (Ps. 78:1-7). Understanding the unique characteristics of each generation will aid us in our mentoring relationships.

In 2011, a group of leaders and I attended a leadership event. The host said this was the first time that five generations would be involved in the workplace at once. He expounded on the challenges as well as opportunities that arose from the differences. Here are some generational descriptors, according to Executive Diversity Services, Inc., that provide insight into generational differences.

There are the Veterans (1930-1945) who have experienced The Great Depression, a war that was supported by the general population, and that was "won" because everyone pulled together and sacrificed for success. As a result, they are conservative, financially prudent, and loyal to their employers

Baby Boomers (1946-1964) have experienced the benefits of financial growth following the war that led to large numbers of homeowners and college graduates due to the GI bill. These experiences have resulted in a generation that is ambitious, exhibits a strong work ethic, and are loyal to careers and employers.

Generation X (1965-1976) experienced both parents working to achieve financial success. This was the first generation of "latch key kids" who took care of chores and themselves before parents came home from work. This experience had led to a generation that is often highly independent.

Generation Y (1977-1994), reared in a similar environment as Generation Xers, but with a different parenting style (e.g. timeouts, not spanking), has also grown up with rapid communication via the internet, and understands what is happening socially and politically around the globe and to the environment. These experiences have resulted in a generation that is described as extremely conscious of the global environment; open minded and accepting of differences in race, gender, ethnicity, sexual orientation, socially conscious, and concerned with personal safety.

Gen Z (1995 and after) grew up slowly as teens, and were late bloomers when it came to acquiring a job and driver's license. Because of this, they are joining the workplace with less experience in independent decision making. But they pride themselves on wanting to make a difference in the world and are adept at learning new things via technology.

There will always be differences amongst past, current and future generations—this is normal. Yet one of the most obvious differences today is the knowledge and use of technology via smartphones. Young adults experience so much of their lives through their phones. In their book *Faith for Exiles*, David Kinnaman and Mark Matlock estimated that the typical fifteen- to twenty-three year old spends 2,767 hours per year looking at screens. This has resulted in more loneliness, depression, and anxiety according to researcher Jean Twenge. These stats only reveal the need for face-to-face interaction with a mentor who cares.

At the age of thirty, Jesus began His ministry (Luke 3:23) and was considered a mature adult. He was empowered by the Holy Spirit (Luke 4:1) and was able to articulate what He was going to do with His life (Luke 4:18-19).

His life offers great insight for mentoring.

> And Jesus, walking by the Sea of Galilee, saw two brothers, Simon called Peter, and Andrew his brother, casting a net into the sea; for they were fishermen. Then He said to them, "Follow Me, and I will make you fishers of men." They immediately left their nets

and followed Him. Going on from there, He saw two other brothers, James the son of Zebedee, and John his brother, in the boat with Zebedee their father, mending their nets. He called them. (Matthew 4:18-21)

Historically, a rabbi would begin to take on students that were younger than him. The Bible doesn't tell the ages of the disciples, but there are certain age indicators from a cultural and historical context. For example, those following a rabbi started as early as twelve, but were usually less than twenty years old. They were often unmarried, as a Jewish man received a wife after the age of eighteen. Peter is the only disciple who had a wife according to Scripture (Matt. 8:14). Jesus called His disciples little children in John 13:33, which would be insulting to an adult man thirty or older.

For this younger generation, key motivators are "mission" and "impact." A recent report found that seventy-three percent of Millennials had volunteered for a non-profit organization. Jesus believed in and invested in the younger generation.

In Jewish culture, children were able to recite the Torah, the first five books of the Bible. The smartest boys would then go to a rabbi to ask if they could become his disciple. Most of these boys were not chosen and were instead taught a trade. This is where Jesus found His disciples—in the trade taught to them by their fathers. These are the young men Jesus hand-picked, not the best and brightest in the temple.

When a rabbi chose a disciple, he was saying, "I believe in you; you can become like me." In John's account of Peter meeting Jesus, He said in John 1:47, "You are Simon the son of Jonah. You shall be called Cephas." (when translated means a stone). As much as we may think we're different, we all have something in common—we want someone to believe that we can become more, and do great things. As mentors, one of the greatest things we can do is believe in those we mentor. Jesus reached out to His disciples, believed in them, and it made all the difference in their lives.

Many years ago, I was a part of a group of young ministers from the Los Angeles area that flew to Tulsa, Oklahoma, to attend a conference called "Azusa." The conference was attended by thousands and thousands of people from around the country. It was an amazing few days filled with great teaching, worship, meeting new people, and encountering God's presence.

During the final night of the conference, there was a tangible presence of God that filled the auditorium. I distinctly recall weeping. Many others did as well. Even the most unemotional person would've shed tears in that environment. It was in that moment of brokenness before the Lord that I heard Him say to me, "I'm going to use young people." This was encouraging to me as a young minister, but I realized it was a word to encourage all young people.

I don't believe the Lord spoke this to me to discriminate against those who are middle-aged or older. I received it for me personally and to encourage the young people whom I mentor that God wants to use them.

Brain Drain

One of the challenges threatening to undermine the continued growth of our economy is "Brain Drain," when knowledge drains out of organizations because of retirements and other turnovers. The term "Brain Drain" was first coined by the Royal Society to describe the immigration of scientists and technologists to America from post-war Europe. The term has been broadened to define the mass immigration of technically-skilled people from one country to another.

As Baby Boomers retire, there is the looming reality of a 'Boomer Brain Drain' without the corresponding brain-gain. Churches and companies will face this over the next few years with increasing intensity.

According to the Bureau of Labor Statistics, the average large company will lose thirty to forty percent of its workforce over the next five to ten years. Since Gen-Xers are already in the workforce, the replacement for the Boomer mass exodus will be Millennial professionals. Recruiting and retaining them is going to be very competitive.

An important key for building a relationship with the Millennial generation is the transfer of knowledge. If Boomer professionals do not attract and connect with this generation, we'll lose more than just a familiar work environment.

There are two types of knowledge. I'm referring to tacit and explicit knowledge. Tacit knowledge passed down from one generation to the next cannot be over emphasized. Explicit knowledge is formal and is written down. Tacit knowledge is the kind of knowledge that is difficult to transfer from one person to another via media. When we have tacit knowledge we are often not even aware we possess it, let alone aware of the value in transferring it to others.

In learning to speak a language, tacit knowledge plays a major role. I don't remember learning English, nor do I remember any formal details of teaching my children English. The information was tacit—simply passed on. One of the key connectors in the transfer was the relationship I had with my parents and the relationship I had with my own children.

After Jesus assembled everyone, He left them with another member of the Godhead who would be like Him—the Holy Spirit. One of the results of the Spirit's outpouring in Acts 2:17 is that old men (including women) will "dream dreams." God never intended for you to stop dreaming, even as you grow older. You are to dream until you take in your last breath.

I remember visiting my best friend's mom (I'll call her Susan) in the hospital as she slowly deteriorated from cancer. As we spoke, she told me something I never knew. Susan said to me that all of her life she wanted to work with children, but never did. I felt like she was sharing a part of her dream with me. Sadly, Susan passed away without ever experiencing her dream. I'm grateful she shared that secret of her heart with me, so I can now share with you and encourage your heart.

You are not too old to dream. The older you get, the better you should be dreaming: in high definition with surround sound!

Get started on your heart's dream. Don't allow procrastination to paralyze your purpose. Write it down, talk to the right people to give you counsel, pray, create timelines, hire a coach, and then act.

My pastor, Bayless Conley, wrote in one of his books that if your dream can be fulfilled in your lifetime you're dreaming too small. Just as you transfer knowledge to the next generation, the same mindset should be had with your dream. Dispense your dream to others younger than you, because a dream must never die with the dreamer.

Dispense your dream to others younger than you, because a dream must never die with the dreamer

King David had it in his heart to build a house for God, but he gave that dream away to Solomon so it could be fulfilled. And Solomon fulfilled it in the grandest way possible.

Reflection Questions

1. How can you know if a mentee truly wants help?

2. How can you prepare yourself to believe in your mentee?

3. What can you do to learn about the generation you are mentoring?

4. How can you practically assist your mentee with their dreams?

5. What are tangible ways you can encourage your mentee to cultivate their dream?

My Prayer...

Lord, give me largeness of heart to dream big and help others to do the same.

Key No. 8

Models for Mentoring

I n this chapter, I would like to share a message from my heart with you as a mentor. Please understand this idea of mentoring is more than a suggestion; I believe it is a divine call. The world in which we live today is in desperate need of leadership—leadership in our homes, in our schools, in our communities, and in our world.

Many of you would agree with me when I say the world we live in today is vastly different from the world we grew up in as young children, teenagers, and young adults. Our children and teenagers today need caring people of character who are willing to invest themselves in the greatest commodity that our world has to offer, and that is the life of another human being. Whenever a person invests financially, they do so with the idea of getting a return on their investment (ROI); in essence they want to make more money in the future than what they actually invested in the present. When it comes to mentoring, the investment into the lives of others in the present will produce a far more lasting return on our investment into who a person can become and the quality of life he can live. Investment in others will always be greater than any monetary investment.

I realize some of you reading this book have had extreme difficulty in your life and do not feel whole enough to help someone else. You feel like you're in such desperate need that there is nothing you could do for anyone else. I encourage you to get the help you need now, because your trials can lead to teachable moments in the future.

Investment in others will always be greater than any monetary investment

Remember that all of our help comes from the Lord. If you look to Him first, He will indeed help you in ways that will astound you and aid you in moving forward in life. Do not dismiss yourself from being able to help someone else because of your past difficulties.

In 1 Chronicles 12:32 it says, "the sons of Issachar who had understanding of the times, to know what Israel ought to do." I've read that suicide is now the second leading cause of death for all Americans ages ten to thirty-four, according to the Centers for Disease Control and Prevention (CDC). The CDC also reports that the U.S. suicide rate has increased thirty percent since the year 2000 and tripled for teen girls. It is difficult when you lose a beloved family member or friend because it hurts. But when someone takes their life, it adds a deeper dimension of grief and personal trauma to the family and friends who remain. So the question is, "what are we to do?" One of the things we can do is to be a mentor to others. Invest your life and what you have learned into the lives of others.

Many of you are approaching, or have arrived, at the middle age of life. This is an interesting stage in your life because you're not as young as you used to be, but you're not old either. It's the half-time of your life. You had and still have a great career, you've accomplished some great things individually and in your family, and you've earned your dues. You've gone through some battles and have the scars to show it. You've fallen on your face and gotten back up many times. You deal with the thoughts of "does my life matter?" and "What am I going to do with the rest of my life?" You have feelings of wanting to be acknowledged because you have sacrificed, even if your life is not showing all the rewards of your sacrifice. And it would be nice if someone said "thank you" or acknowledged how you helped them, but maybe that hasn't occurred.

I wonder if these thoughts ever crossed your mind: "I still matter"; "I'm not too old". There has been a surge in our society to slow down or reverse aging and return to youth. I'm grateful for new advances and discoveries when it comes to eating healthier, living better, and exercising. There are surgical procedures and anti-aging creams that can slow down this process, but the truth is we're still aging. All of us want to make a difference and leave our footprints in the sands of time. All of us want to influence current change for the better, as well as future change for the best. Mentoring is one of the ways where you make yourself younger, especially when you are involved in the lives of young people—you don't get old because they keep you young.

I now want to give you some different methods or models of mentoring. In my neighborhood there are many homes, yet the homes are not all built and designed the same way. As I walk down the street, I see some homes that, although different in style, are designed exactly alike. They're all homes, but the models are different. This concept exists with mentoring as well.

The first model is called the One-on-One Model. This is the basic model of mentoring where there is one mentor and one mentee. There is a relationship that has been established, and connection, growth, and development take place in this relationship. This is what occurred between the wise sage, Mentor, and the son of Odysseus, Telemachus. This is the type of model that occurred between Cardale and myself and the model I primarily use. In this model, there is a deep sense of value by the mentee because of the personal attention and time given by the mentor.

The second model is called the Multiple Mentor Model. This model occurs when the mentor has more than one mentee or is mentoring multiple mentees at the same time. If the mentor has the capacity, he/she might mentor several mentees simultaneously, but meet with them at different times. Another application of this model takes place when the mentor meets with a group of mentees, perhaps three to five. This would be considered a small group. This model is effective because of the mutual sharing that occurs in a group setting (which enhances learning) and the feel of community that is experienced by the mentees. The mentor is still looked to as the leader or the facilitator of the group, but learning takes place as the mentor shares and as the mentees share as well. This was the model Jesus used with His twelve disciples. As a mentor, this model provides the opportunity to duplicate and multiply what can be imparted to your mentees.

The third model is called the Joint Mentoring Model. This model is described as when a mentor and his mentee join together with another mentor and mentee. It's basically the one-on-one mentoring model, doubled. This creates another small group dynamic which is very helpful for youth and young adults because of their attraction and wiring for community. The mentor does not have to share everything with his mentees or the other mentees because another mentor is present to add insight and value to the conversation. Additionally, the mutual learning and sharing of the mentees who are present enhances the growth and development of all.

The fourth model is called Organizational Mentoring. This model of mentoring is a culture that can be created (and actually should be created) in every workplace in the world. If every organization and business adopted this kind of culture, there would be enormous individual and team growth, which would affect company growth. Why? It's simple. Every person wants to grow into their full potential and mentoring facilitates this. This culture also ensures ongoing training in every department and with every position. The fear of losing your job can be replaced with the excitement of training someone else to do your job because that is part of your job.

This model works best with 1) incoming employees; 2) those who are stepping into new positions; and 3) those nearing the end of their time or career at the company, or who are moving on to another position elsewhere.

There has been a phenomenon that has occurred in many corporations called "brain drain" (see chapter 7). This happens when long-time employees of twenty to thirty years begin nearing retirement. They possess the educational background, aptitude, ongoing training, and experience that has sustained them decade after decade, but as they approach the door to leave the company and walk into retirement, they take with them all the years of knowledge, understanding, and skill that incoming employees do not possess. The brain wealth that they leave with drains the company's new employees of that wealth. It should not be this way. The brain wealth they possess will be gained by the company's up and coming employees as this model is applied.

The fifth model is called **Church Mentoring**. This model should also be a culture that is adopted in every church around the world. The reason why this should be more prevalent in the church than any place else is because Jesus gave us the commission to go into all the world and make disciples of every nation. So, we have a mandate to teach and pass on what we've learned so that others can learn of the Lord and serve Him as well. I believe if we can model this culture in the church, then we can fulfill His commission more effectively. Please see Appendix A for Best Practices for training.

Pastor Jeffrey and Angela Rachmat are pastors of a great church in Jakarta, Indonesia, called Jakarta Praise Community Church. While speaking to our Cottonwood staff one day,

Pastor Jeffrey shared how at his church, they have at least two to three replacements ready for each key position in his church.

If a person can no longer serve at his position, another is ready to step in. That does not happen by accident, but with intentionality, vision, training, and mentoring.

Here are three different options of how this could work in your church:

- The men's ministry and women's ministry taking on a mentoring role with men in the church and women in the church.

- The men's ministry and women's ministry taking on a mentoring role with the young adults in the church.

- The young adults taking on a mentoring role with high school-aged boys and girls to mentor them with a specific curriculum.

The sixth model is called Community Mentoring. This model of mentoring focuses on a number of areas, such as local middle schools, local high schools, foster care youth who have aged out of the system, and other organizations that exist in various communities.

This model applies when a church or organization partners with one of the aforementioned entities to provide mentoring for those who need or desire it.

I believe the desired and best context for mentoring will always be face to face. Yet, we must be open and willing to use the various platforms of technology that enable us to communicate and connect. Therefore, take advantage of FaceTime, video calls, and Zoom conferencing as viable options when necessary.

Reflection Questions

1. In what ways do you consider mentoring to be a divine call in your life?

2. What can you do to incorporate mentoring into your life today?

3. Think of a young person in your life right now—what are three practical ways you could invest in them to cultivate increase?

4. How can God use your challenges, struggles, and victories to help your mentee?

5. What models of mentoring do you see yourself participating in, and, most importantly, how?

My Prayer...

Father, I ask You for a constant renewal of strength and the wisdom to implement the best ways to mentor others.

Key No. 9

Mentoring Your Successor to Succeed

One of my favorite animated movies of all time is *The Lion King*. Without exaggeration, I've probably seen the movie in theaters, on DVD, and on stage at least fifteen times. I love the storyline, which centers around two main characters—Mufasa, the current Lion King, and Simba, the future Lion King. At its heart, the movie is about succession. In one scene Mufasa speaks to his son Simba and mentions something called the 'Circle of Life,' which happens to be the theme song of the movie. In the chorus of the song, performed by Carmen Twilley and composed by Sir Elton John, it states:

> *It's the circle of life*
> *And it moves us all*
> *Through despair and hope*
> *Through faith and love*
> *'Til we find our place*
> *On the path unwinding*
> *In the circle*
> *The circle of life*

It's an inspiring song with a clear message. Mufasa endeavored to prepare Simba for the day when he would no longer be king and Simba would take his rightful place as the king of the jungle. It was a lot for the young lion cub to digest, but what his dad told him came to pass. He did become the next Lion King.

When it comes to mentoring, one of the obvious applications we must consider is the one of mentoring our successor. As creatures of habit, we can easily picture ourselves in a certain position, but find it hard to envision ourselves out of that position. When you have been in a position for a long time, you develop deep emotional, relational and experiential roots. These roots are called commitment, sacrifice, skill, learning, mistakes, maturity, and growth. Your identity has been shaped by this role and the relationships that have been formed over years, relationships that become like family. Yet, in the deepest part of your heart you know that the edge you once had, the excitement for the position and all that it entails, has been on a slow decline for some time. You just haven't wanted to face the facts because you don't know what's next or what you would do if you left your position or the company.

This is not an easy task for a leader. Even when it's the right thing to do and is done intentionally and strategically, it's still hard for a leader to release the influence, notoriety, title, visibility, and perks of a position.

But life is like that circle mentioned from *The Lion King*. Before you stepped into your position, someone was doing what you did. And before they stepped in to that position, someone else did it before them. Now you are faced with the reality that your time in this position will come to an end. This doesn't mean that your life is over and your purpose is complete; it only means that you must begin to think of how you stepped into this position, how someone gave you a chance, and begin to prepare yourself to give another person a chance. You must mentor your successor. This is your next step before you leave your post.

It demonstrates your selfless forethought for the continued success of your church or organization. One could think, "I've done my time. I paid my dues. I'm out of here!" But that is not the appropriate mindset of a Christian, a leader, or a mentor. Whenever you depart a position or a place, always leave it better than when you first came and set up the person taking over so he or she is poised to march into the future. Mentoring your successor will ensure that these things are able to happen.

In the Bible, there are a few individuals who have something in common. Here's the list: Joshua, Elisha, Solomon, and the disciples of Jesus. What do all of these individuals have in common? They were all successors to someone else, and the person for whom they succeeded took the time to mentor them. How would they have fared if they were not mentored to succeed? Would Joshua have taken over Jericho and led the children of Israel into the promised land? Would Elisha have worked twice as many miracles as Elijah and helped diminish the worship of Baal? Would Solomon have built the temple if

> *Whenever you depart a position or a place, always leave it better than when you first came*

David hadn't provided from his own treasury and given him the plans that the Holy Spirit gave to him?

Would we profess and possess this faith in Jesus Christ if He had not mentored His disciples for three and a half years? Things would have been different in the lives of all of these individuals had they not been tutored in the tasks they would inherit one day. Some of you who are reading this have had the experience of stepping into a position or role without any mentoring or training at all. You had to fly by the seat of your pants or quickly learn the job. I too have that kind of the story, but allow me to share the story of how I mentored one of my successors.

My story begins in 1990, when I enrolled in Bible college at Cottonwood Christian Center. I graduated in June 1992 and was asked to come back and teach in the fall of 1992. I was then voted to be alumni president. Next, I became the dean of men in the school while continuing to teach. I took over the leadership of the college in November 2003 and officially became the executive director of the Bible college in January 2004. After this, the Lord placed a young man named Garrett Sederholm on my heart to be a part of the team. In 2006 I hired Garrett, a graduate of our school, in a part-time capacity. He was faithful, had a heart to serve, was teachable, and I recognized his calling to preach the gospel. Garrett continued to grow and develop and began to do some teaching in the school in addition to carrying other responsibilities.

There came a time when it became clear to me that Garrett was next in line to lead the school. In order to help you understand what this process could look like, I will outline my process of mentoring Garrett to take over the leadership of school.

First, I began to think of the Scriptures where this model was repeated over and over in the Old Testament, as well as in the New Testament. I began to think of the future and realized I would not be the leader of the school forever. A predominant thought I had was to mentor Garrett to take over the school. I knew it was the right thing to do and it could be done without there being a negative reason for me no longer being the leader.

Second, I began to have conversations with my pastor and other leaders in school about the idea of Garrett being prepared to take over the school.

Third, I had a conversation with Garrett to find out what was in his heart. We already had a great relationship, as we had lots of fun talking, yet there was a mutual respect and appreciation for one another. I was blessed to hear Garrett tell me that God had spoken to him before about leading a Bible school. Wow! How about that? It's amazing how God orchestrates the calling and purpose in our lives. From this point, we had candid conversations about my role as a leader, the responsibilities I had, and what that looked like in the context of our church. Garrett would ask questions and listen.

Fourth, I sat down and wrote down all the things I wanted to teach Garrett that would be essential for him to know as leader of the school. With that, I attached a timeline for these things to be imparted to him through time spent communicating. I am a very methodical person and I like to think through things before acting; some may call this being cautious, but I call it being clear and strategic. There were times when it seemed like it was taking too long from Garrett's perspective, so I would listen and assure him that this is the direction we were going in. I can understand the impatience of waiting for something that is like a dream, but there is a time for every purpose under heaven. During this process, Garrett met his wife. I had the great honor of officiating their wedding.

Fifth, after our conversation of Garrett becoming a leader one day and having continual conversations on that topic, I began to learn more about Garrett and his leadership in the school. I offered him more consistent teaching, more opportunities to be in front of the students, more input in meetings, and a chance to participate in decision-making. I intentionally began to expose him to the unpleasant side of things that came along with leadership. I didn't do this all at once, so as not to overwhelm him, but instead I endeavored to do it progressively, talking through some of the circumstances and decisions.

Sixth, I often shared stories with Garrett so he could understand more about ministry and the demands that would be placed on him, as well as some of the things I'd lived out experientially. The stories were filled with insights, emotion, good wisdom, or lack thereof. Anyone who will be your successor must understand both sides of the position; it's not all glory and glamour. There are hard days, and times when you have to do things you would rather not, but you step up anyway because it's your responsibility.

I asked Garrett for some of his thoughts regarding this idea of "successor-mentoring" based on our relationship. Here are some of the insights he shared with me.

- "You always believed in my God-given potential, even when I failed or when my life was seemingly falling apart."

- "You gave me a lot of grace to grow through immature seasons and mistakes, etc."

- "You shared a lot of life/ ministry experience that went on behind closed doors to equip me for the future."

- "You've always been a genuine friend to me and not just a formal mentor. Ironically, that made you an even better mentor."

In July 2016, at one of our summer trainings for instructors, I officially announced I would be stepping down as the executive director of the leadership college and that Garrett would become the new director. I encouraged the team to embrace his leadership, and then I called him up to the front to lay hands on him and pray for him. Next, I removed my physical presence from the school so he would be the leader all the faculty, staff, volunteers, and students would look to.

I'm proud to know Garrett as a friend and I consider him to be a man of character who loves God, loves his family, and loves people. He is doing an excellent job in leading

Cottonwood College and will take it into a new day. A current and new generation of servant-leaders are being trained to make a difference in the world for Christ.

Reflection Questions

1. Examine your heart—do you sincerely want those replacing you to exceed your success?

2. If you don't know who will fill your shoes, how can you find that person in order to prepare them?

3. In what ways can you help your successor reach their full potential after you've left the position?

4. Whatever stage of life you are in, how can you best facilitate either preparing your successor or preparing yourself to fill another's role?

5. What are some potential pitfalls and stumbling blocks you can help your mentee foresee and prepare for?

My Prayer...

Lord, purge my heart of any pride or selfish motives that would keep me from fully supporting, equipping and rejoicing in my mentee's success!

Key No. 10

The Rewards of Mentoring

Growing up, I can recall how much I enjoyed receiving awards, trophies, certificates, and anything that acknowledged my efforts. Reward is something given in recognition of one's service, effort, or achievement. Receiving honors is an acknowledgment of hard work and dedication in a particular field or endeavor. In many ways, rewards are a symbol of a return on your investment. A future reward can act as a motivator during times when fatigue has set in or when you feel like you hit a wall and wonder if you should just throw in the towel. Suffice it to say rewards are indeed important. God knows the value of rewards and speaks of them throughout Scripture. In eternity, rewards, crowns, and authority are some of the things God has promised for those who faithfully serve Him.

As stated in an earlier chapter, there are costs to mentoring. It takes time and energy to develop a relationship. It requires energy and effort in prayer and even resources into the relationship in order to see it grow. It's not like you're going to receive a trophy, plaque, or certificate for mentoring others. You don't ask for payment for mentoring—it's a philanthropic activity. So what are the rewards for mentoring? If you've ever mentored someone before, you will understand the rewards are not tangible, but intangible. Here are a few rewards of mentoring worthy of mentioning to encourage and inspire you as you mentor others.

The number one reward of mentoring is you get to invest what you've learned and earned over time. Our life experiences are teaching tools not only for us, but also for others. There are things we have learned by trial and error, through blood, sweat, and tears; and there are things we have earned through hard work, focus, and persistence. The right to speak and be heard, the right to certain opportunities and privileges. The right given to one who has endured and has demonstrated longevity. What if your life experiences were measured out in the form of dollars? You would be a billionaire! I can hear some of you thinking right now, "I wish that were the case!" Well, what would you do with one billion USD? There's a lot of things you could think of, but you would probably get to the end of your list and realize you still have millions left. One of the great privileges of having more than you need is you get to give to those who are in need. I believe this is what Paul meant as he echoed the words of Jesus in Acts 20:35: "it is more blessed to give than to receive." Paul refers to the special relationship he had with the Philippian church, calling them his joy and his crown. His reward was in serving them and it was his joy to do so.

The number two reward of mentoring is fruitfulness and multiplication. One of the mandates God gave to mankind in the book of Genesis was to be fruitful and multiply. This of course has application as it relates to procreation, but I believe the meaning is much broader and has more application to our lives. We were designed to be fruitful and for that fruit to be multiplied. When we are not fruitful, we experience frustration, because innately we know there is so much more within us that is not being released and expressed. Mentoring gives us the opportunity to take part in the process of becoming fruitful which is: to sow into someone else's life and to water their lives with knowledge, wisdom, and belief.

I was over my mother's house one day and she invited me to come out to the backyard and look at her tangerine tree. The reason she wanted to show me her tree is because it was abundantly full of tangerines. I had never seen it that bountiful before. She had to hire someone to come and pull all those tangerines down and put them into bags in order to give them away. I don't believe she would've had the same excitement in her voice to show me a tree with little or no fruit. My mother's neighbors were blessed with sweet, juicy, and delicious tangerines because the tree was fruitful.

Jesus said in John 15:16 that He chose and appointed us that we should go and bear fruit, and that our fruit should remain. This affirms the truth conveyed in Genesis that God wants us to be fruitful, and mentoring is a

Mentoring is a practical way to bring forth fruit and watch it multiplied in the life of another

practical way to bring forth fruit and watch it multiplied in the life of another.

The third reward of mentoring is personal fulfillment. Now, we don't mentor just so that we can experience personal fulfillment, but when we mentor *we will* experience personal fulfillment. The definition of fulfillment is "the achievement of something desired, promised or predicted." On the heels of ministering to a broken woman in John 4, Jesus said to His followers, "My food is to do the will of Him who sent me and to finish His work." There was a fulfillment Jesus experienced inwardly that He likened to the satisfaction that one derives from having eaten food. In the context of the story, He actually was physically tired and hungry, but by doing what He was led to do in serving this woman He was fulfilled.

The fourth reward of mentoring is observing the growth and transformation of your mentee's life. When you begin the process of mentoring your mentees, it may be like wet clay on the potter's wheel. But as you continue to sow your time and talent and even treasure into an individual, you will begin to notice God bringing about transformation in their lives. You've heard of the term "metamorphosis"; this describes the process of a caterpillar turning into a beautiful butterfly. The caterpillar eats a lot of food and grows bigger, then goes through a period where it forms a chrysalis or cocoon. The caterpillar will generally stay hidden within this cocoon while the metamorphosis miracle takes place. No one on the outside of the cocoon can see what's going on inside during that five to twenty-one day period. It's worth noting that if a caterpillar is in a harsh environment like a desert, it could take up to three years before it emerges, as it may wait for rain or the right condition. All of a sudden, the cocoon begins to move, then crack, and out of it emerges a creature who can now soar instead of crawl. As mentors we do not get to see the inside of the cocoon, which represents the person's mind and heart—only God sees this miracle! Remember, sometimes those we mentor might be late bloomers and the experiences of their lives have not been easy. It might take a bit more of your patience with their process.

What we do see, depending on how often and how long the mentoring relationship continues, are the outward, visible results of the inward transformation. This, my friend, is a reward.

The final reward of mentoring is simply that of joy. It is the response when any one, two, or all of the above take place in your mentee's life. It can be likened to the elation that young parents feel the first time their child says "da-da" or "ma-ma," or, when the child takes his first steps and begins to walk on his own. The parents begin to laugh, clap, pick the child up and hug him, post pictures on Facebook and Instagram, etc. Even the slightest signs of improvement or development in your mentee that you observe cause a huge smile on the inside of your heart. It reminds me of the sentiment in 3 John 4, which states: "I have no greater joy than to hear that my children walk in the truth."

There is another level and depth of joy which goes beyond the person whom you're mentoring and proceeds to the lives he/she touches and builds. I have listened to several men whom my mentee Garrett has mentored (or is mentoring) share with me how much he has helped them. They genuinely share how he takes time with them and encourages them with the Word in their circumstances, resulting in them being stronger because they listened. I've gone back to the college to teach as a guest speaker from time to time and I sense the effects of Garrett's influence and leadership. I've heard students from their early twenties to their seventies and everyone in between speak with high regard for this man of God. How can I describe to you what I feel? J-O-Y!

In the first year of my marriage to Angel, we became the legal guardians of her youngest brother, Eugene. This came about because of some tough circumstances within the family and his need for stability. He was a quiet thirteen-year-old who had gone through some difficult things as a kid. Angel is the only female sibling, so none of her brothers were excited about me marrying their sister, including young Eugene.

Nonetheless, when presented with this option for Eugene to stay with us, I had to speak to Angel, think, and *really, really* pray. This was our first year of marriage; we had our firstborn daughter, Ja'nay, and we were living in a one-bedroom apartment in Long Beach. If someone were to describe this situation to me and ask for my input, I would probably say don't do it, but as I read these verses, I felt like we were supposed to do it.

> But whoever has this world's goods, and sees his brother
> in need, and shuts up his heart from him, how does the
> love of God abide in him? (1 John 3:17)

Eugene lived with us for the next seven years and then stepped out on his own with a little encouragement (smile). Over the years, Eugene has worked hard, and the area he's invested the most into are his boys, my nephews Ross and Devon. These are two of the most respectable and well-mannered young men I know. They are good young men.

Eugene recently drove a long distance to bring the boys over to visit with my mother, who is in her eighties. Since that visit, my mom has raved about how respectful and delightful Ross and Devon are and how she was blessed to be with them. The credit for them goes to Eugene and their mother, but God gave me the opportunity to influence a young man, albeit my brother in law, and to see his sons is always a joy.

All of these rewards and more will become your experience as you mentor and continue *Helping Others Win*!

Reflection Questions

1. What are some of the costs of being a mentor?

2. What are the joys and rewards of mentoring?

3. Expound on some life experiences you've had that could help your mentee.

4. What is your role during the time of metamorphosis, when you cannot see what God is doing within your mentee?

5. How have you seen fruitfulness and multiplication through the lives of those you've touched?

My Prayer...

Lord, thank you for the honor of being called to mentor and for the matchless joy of Helping Others Win!

Questions and Answers About Mentoring

1. **Question**: Who can be a mentor?

    Answer: Anyone who cares for others, is relational, and believes he can help another grow can be a mentor. Eighteen years old is a recommended age to begin mentoring.

2. **Question**: If I'm not mentoring my own children should I mentor someone else?

    Answer: As a parent, you are naturally in the place to mentor your children, although it may not appear to be formal to you. So, yes you can mentor other young people.

3. **Question**: How much time will I have to commit to mentoring?

    Answer: You must review your weekly schedule based on your personal time, your work responsibilities, family responsibilities, and other organizational responsibilities, then see what you can reasonably and comfortably commit to. You must be realistic with the time you schedule to commit. Start with connecting once a month.

4. **Question**: What should you know prior to becoming a mentor?

   Answer: Mentors should be knowledgeable about building rapport and opportunities to support their mentee in a variety of ways.

5. **Question**: Any advice for new mentors for their first one-on-one meeting together?

   Answer: Yes. Mentors should enter the meeting with an open mind and room for flexibility. The mentor should be ready to listen and provide a safe place for the mentee.

6. **Question**: What books should I read in preparing to be a mentor?

   Answer: *The Miracle of Mentoring* by Bayless Conley; *Mentoring: Biblical, Theological and Practical Perspectives* by Wm. B. Erdmans; *Mentoring: Confidence in Finding a Mentor and Becoming One* by

Bob Biehl; *Mentoring to Develop Disciples and Leaders* by John Malison.

7. **Question**: Where can I get more coaching on mentoring?

    Answer: You can go to www.mentoring.org to seek more training. Speak with those in your circle of relationships who have mentored or are currently mentoring others. Check kennethmulkey.com for online courses.

8. **Question**: What are the best ways to communicate with your mentee?

    Answer: The best way to communicate with your mentee is always face-to-face, but utilize all forms of communication such as phone calls, texts, FaceTime, e-mail, Zoom conferencing, etc. The most important factor is that your communication be consistent and unrushed.

9. **Question**: How much access should your mentee have to your family?

    Answer: I think the best answer for this question is based on the length of time in the relationship with your mentee and your level of comfort in bringing your mentee around your family. Any access is a result of trust, and trust is always earned over time. Therefore, let some time build up and allow the relationship to develop before you offer too much access. Minimally, your mentee will need your phone number, social media name, and email if used.

10. **Question**: If I'm mentoring a young person, do I need to meet his or her parents first?

Answer: Yes, it would be the best practice particularly if they are under eighteen years of age. It would be wise to meet them even if they are older than eighteen, but still living with their parents for the purpose of knowledge and accountability.

11. **Question**: What if the mentee I have is older than me; will that be a problem?

Answer: If your mentee is older than you, yet has agreed to become your mentee, there should not be a problem. His agreement to be your mentee suggests that he believes you can help him to grow.

12. **Question**: What are the differences in mentoring someone who is younger than you, your same age, or older than you?

Answer: Besides the age differences or similarities, the differences will be levels of maturity and experience.

Mentoring can be mostly done by someone who is older; however, if someone who is younger has a high level of maturity and responsibility, as well as knowledge, that person will be an effective mentor.

13. **Question**: Should a man mentor a man and woman only mentor a woman? Why or why not?

   Answer: I believe that mentoring can take place indirectly, and the gender differences will not be an issue. However, the pattern of Scripture primarily shows men mentoring men and teaches that women should mentor women. We see this modeled time and time again, whereas we do not see direct mentoring of the opposite sex modeled for us. I believe this model safeguards us from unnecessary temptations and other possible distractions.

14. **Question**: How do I maintain proper boundaries when mentoring the son of a single woman and I am a single man, or vice versa?

   Answer: The key in maintaining proper boundaries is to first realize your purpose in mentoring this parent's son or daughter. You are in a relationship with him or her to serve them and have acquired the trust of the parent in order to do so. Stay focused. I would recommend setting proper boundaries beforehand so that you can maintain them. Share these boundaries with another mentor-friend who can regularly ask if you are adhering to the boundaries.

15. **Question**: Is it best to mentor someone from your same ethnicity and culture?

Answer: There may be an advantage when you mentor someone of the same ethnicity and culture, but Jesus commissioned us to make disciples of all nations (people groups) which would suggest that we would be in relationship with those who are not of the same ethnicity and culture as us. It is best to mentor someone who wants to be mentored.

16. **Question**: What if the mentee is inconsistent and does not want to be mentored?

Answer: The mentee must desire to be mentored in order for the mentoring to be beneficial for his or her life. If this is not the case, there is no need to force mentoring upon anyone who doesn't desire it.

17. **Question**: What if my mentee is very introverted, doesn't talk much, and does not ask any questions?

Answer: If this is the type of personality your mentee has, or they are behaving in this manner, it may not mean that he doesn't want mentoring. If you sense this individual wants to be mentored, and is diligent in your meeting times and in completing assignments, etc., keep going. Do not be deterred from pursuing the mentoring relationship. You might be a catalyst who will help this person to open up more and trust, if that was an issue of the past.

18. **Question**: How will I know if I'm unable to actually help my mentee to grow? What are the signs? What do I look for?

Answer: In any relationship, there is normally a connection based on commonality or common interest. This connection often creates a chemistry in the relationship. Sometimes that chemistry between a mentor and mentee is non-existent. This may not mean that the person does not desire mentoring, nor does it mean that you are not a great mentor. It might just mean that you may not be the right fit for this mentee. This happens in classrooms between teachers and students, coaches and players all the time, so it's possible it could happen in this context as well.

19. **Question**: How do you stay excited and enthusiastic about mentoring when you aren't seeing any observable growth?

Answer: You have to revisit your "why" as it relates to mentoring. The why is your bigger picture, your vision of why you are mentoring. The Bible tells us that we need to stir ourselves up—in other words, get yourself going and motivate yourself. This is something we must apply in mentoring because we cannot rely on the mentee to provide our motivation for us. If your mentee wants to be mentored by you, let that be motivation enough.

20. **Question**: How do I handle my insecurities if my mentee has more education or better employment than I? Can I still mentor him?

Answer: You handle your insecurities by not allowing your insecurities to overwhelm you and cause you to disqualify yourself as a mentor. This is why the exercises in chapter three were so important for you to do—because they revealed just how much you have to offer someone. A higher salary or better job does not give someone more value than the other person.

21. **Question**: Do adults need mentoring if they have never had a mentor before?

Answer: Any adult can benefit from a mentoring relationship if there is a desire and a realization that they need mentoring in specific areas and in certain seasons of their life.

22. **Question**: What happens if the mentoring relationship has to be discontinued before its agreed upon time of conclusion?

    Answer: Have a conversation with your mentee to determine when might be a better time to continue in the mentoring relationship. This is only a matter of having an open and honest conversation. Set up a transition time to discontinue the mentoring relationship, but continue as a friend.

23. **Question**: What is the most tactful way to end a mentoring relationship when it's obvious that it is not working?

    Answer: Set a time to have a conversation with your mentee to discuss your concerns and to see if there had been concerns on the side of your mentee. Remember, sometimes the chemistry is not a fit and if it doesn't, it's better to acknowledge it through conversation and remain friends. This is better than attempting to continue to make mentoring happen, which could do more damage.

24. **Question**: If I engage in the joint mentoring model and another mentor seems to take all the talking time, how do I handle that situation?

Answer: Set up a time to have a private conversation to discuss your concern with the other mentor. Give this mentor the opportunity to respond to your observations. This mentor may be unaware of what he's doing. We all have blind spots. I would then see how he responds to this concern. Does he seem unaware? Is he apologetic? Agree upon a solution with follow-up conversations for accountability.

25. **Question:** Can I mentor someone who has deep emotional issues or suffers with a mental illness?

    Answer: I believe you can mentor someone in either of these conditions. It depends few things: first, the degree and/or depth of the mentee's condition, and second, the mentor's emotional capacity and strength to help the mentee grow. Another consideration is that the mentee might need a person who can be trusted, a listening ear, and a kind and encouraging voice. This may be the mentoring goal in this relationship.

26. **Question:** What if the mentee needs counseling; what do I do?

    Answer: A mentor is not considered a professional counselor, but does provide advice and thoughts to help guide the mentee. If it is discovered that the depths of the mentee's problems are beyond your capacity to properly advise the mentee, then it is your responsibility to point the mentee in the direction of counseling or therapy that may be needed.

27. **Question**: Are there materials I could use to help me begin a mentoring culture in my organization or school?

Answer: I do not know of any current materials that could assist you in beginning a mentoring culture. There are consultants and coaches who can assist in this endeavor.

28. **Question**: Do you know of any organizations that have a mentoring culture?

Answer: I'm sure there are many organizations and churches that have a mentoring culture. In chapter eight, I mentioned a church called Jakarta Praise Community Church in Jakarta, Indonesia.

29. **Question**: Do you have to be financially stable to be a mentor?

Answer: A mentor does not need to be financially stable to help guide someone. Mentoring is about planting a seed, no matter if the seed grows or not. Knowledge is power and kindness goes a long way. Money cannot replace the bond and relationship produced by sharing and caring for another person.

30. **Question**: Should a mentor try to change their mentee?

     Answer: A mentor's role is not to change anyone, but to guide and coach in the right direction. If you have a positive influence, then the mentee will move and make their own changes in the right direction.

31. **Question**: Can you mentor someone who doesn't have the same religious beliefs?

     Answer: Mentoring is about building healthy relationships. If you share the same beliefs, then it's a plus, but it shouldn't make a difference. Lead by example and let the mentee see the good in you.

32. **Question**: What challenges can you face with mentoring?

     Answer: Mentoring can create various challenges including attachment, negative emotional ties, frustration, judgment, and not seeing your efforts making a change or a difference. It's possible that a mentee may not take your advice or apply the tools you've suggested.

33. **Question**: What if your eighteen-year-old mentee shares he/she has been physically or sexually abused in the past?

Answer: Thank your mentee for sharing this information, then assure them they are safe with you. Acknowledge how hard that must have been to go through. Ask questions to obtain more facts and listen empathetically. If your mentee is currently unsafe, help them find a safe place. Consult your local Child Protective Services (CPS) and your state laws regarding this.

34. **Question:** What if my mentee is not learning the prescribed knowledge and skills of his new position?

Answer: If your mentee is not absorbing the necessary information for the new position, have a talk with him. Find out how things are going personally and what their concerns are about this new position. Determine practical ideas to aid improvement. Re-state and reset the goals and objectives based on the time remaining in the mentoring process. Meet with your direct report to whom you're responsible for mentoring your mentee.

35. **Question:** How do you avoid burnout as a mentor?

Answer: The answer to this question cannot be given in a sentence of two, so here are my complete answers to assist you in avoiding burnout.

1. <u>Maintain self-care</u>: Keep your spiritual, emotional, social, and physical tanks full. Get enough rest on a regular basis and have fun.

2. <u>Avoid mentoring beyond your capacity</u>: If you have a capacity for two mentees at a time, that's great. Do not allow your compassionate heart to compel you to take on three more mentees when, logistically, you can't.

3. <u>Realize mentoring can be draining</u>: As a mentor, you're in a position of giving. Some mentees may have greater need and demand on you than others. Notice when this is happening and pace yourself.

4. <u>Set proper boundaries</u>: This is a requirement for a healthy mentoring relationship. Without boundaries, the mentee may take your kindness and availability to an extreme.

Appendix A

Church Mentoring Model Best Practices

The following are recommended best practices to implement and execute the Church Mentoring Model within your church. These best practices are given in a prioritized and systematic order to create and cultivate a mentoring culture in your church. As you prayerfully meet, discuss, and design this model amongst your leadership team, you may arrive at some practices not listed. This is normal as you begin to think through the specific and unique dynamics of your congregation. Add these new ideas into your process in order to arrive on the best practices with which your team will build this model.

1. The leadership team must create a clear vision statement regarding mentoring within the church. If it does not exist in the vision, then it must be one of the core values of the church in order to be created and sustained.

2. Determine the organizational structure of this model. Perhaps it will be led by a director, with coaches

beneath him. Then, various department leaders report to a specific coach for counsel, accountability and other situations that may arise.

3. Develop the criteria for those who will mentor (the following are examples):

    A faithful member in good standing with the church
    A contributor to the work of the church
    Completed membership classes
    Served for one year in the church
    At least eighteen years of age

4. Develop the standards and guidelines for behavior and conduct of those who will mentor consistent with biblical, ethical, and moral standards of professionalism.

5. Provide training for all mentors before being allowed to mentor.

6. An application must be completed which includes three letters of recommendation along with an interview by the director or a coach.

7. Local and state background checks must be done.

8. A parental agreement must be signed for mentees less than eighteen years of age.

The parent and child should be clear on what to expect from the mentoring relationship.

Ethical clauses regarding relationships with single parents of the mentee who is a minor must clearly stated.

9. Monthly evaluations of each mentor are to be done by the coaches and quarterly evaluations of the coaches are to be done by the director.

10. All of the above must be carried out in prayer, from selecting mentors to selecting the matches between mentors and mentees.

Bibliography

Blanchard, Ken, *The Servant Leader*, (Nashville: Thomas Nelson, 2003), 42.

Bureau of Labor Statistics, "Employment Projections", September 4, 2019. www.bls.gov. https://www.cdc.gov/nchs/products/databriefs/db330.htm

Centers for Disease Control and Prevention, "Suicide Mortality in the United States, 1999–2017," November 2018.

Clever Magazine, "Humor Archive , Vol. II", Accessed May 27, 2020. https://www.clevermag.com/humor/humorarchII.htm.

Conner, Mark, *Transforming Your Church*, (United Kingdom: Sovereign World Ltd.), p. 182.

Gonzales, Laurence *Deep Survival: Who Lives, Who Dies, and Why*, (New York: W.W. Norton & Company), 71.

John, Elton, *Circle of Life* by Tim Rice. Carmen Twillie, Lebo M, vocalists, track 1 on *The Lion King: Original Motion Picture Soundtrack*. Recorded April 1994, Disney/Mercury, CD, vinyl record.

McCarl, Jay "The One Word Telegram," July 25, 2016, https://jaymccarl.com/2016/07/25/the-one-word-telegram/.

National Service, "Mentoring in America: A Summary of New Research", Accessed May 27, 2020.https://www.nationalservice.gov/pdf/06_0503_mentoring_factsheet.pdf

See Other Books By Author

About the Author

Kenneth Mulkey has been preaching, pastoring and equipping people to serve God for over thirty years. His passion is to see others grow and pursue their God-given purpose.

He is a long time, teaching pastor at Cottonwood Church and oversees the pastoral care of the congregation, where he is affectionately known as "PK".

Thanks to his engaging and humorous delivery, Kenneth speaks locally and internationally, while coaching pastors and leaders in personal and developmental strategies. His book, Run to Win, Finding Your Lane and Finishing, is a resource that aids individuals and small groups in discovering their purpose.

Connect with Kenneth

Facebook: Kenneth Mulkey
Instagram: @ Kenneth_Mulkey
Twitter: @KennethMulkey

CPSIA information can be obtained
at www.ICGtesting.com
Printed in the USA
FSHW020658220920
73852FS